THE DEATH OF ATHEISM

STEPHEN J. FRANEY

FIRST PRINT EDITION

PUBLISHED IN TUCSON, ARIZONA

U.S.A.

PUBLISHING

ISBN–10: 0615570755
ISBN–13: 978–0–615–57075–4

DEDICATION

I would like to dedicate my book to my mom and dad. Thanks for being there. With special thanks to Catherine and Fred Haskell for forcing the book out of the closet.

CONTENTS

THE DEATH OF ATHEISM

What I intend to do in this book is fill up "forever" for you, and I believe you will find that there is only one thing that's been happening forever, and one thing only, and that is, God's been happening, and God alone. Happy reading!

You can't take God out of the equation, because God IS the equation.

Stephen J. Franey

CHAPTER 1

WHO ME?

Allow me to introduce myself. My name is Steve Franey and I drive a taxi in Tucson, Arizona. Impressed? Well, you might as well be, because my life doesn't get anymore exciting than this. After getting a degree in Philosophy in 1977, I have spent most of my life working at low-paying, mediocre jobs that end up going nowhere. I am a man without wealth, without a career, without credentials, without any great achievements to call his own. I am just a simple man who lives alone.

So how could someone like me—a nobody—have anything worthwhile to share with the rest of the world? In all candor, maybe I don't. Then again, maybe I do. Only time will tell.

As dull and uneventful as my outer life appears to be, my inner life is a different story altogether. This is where I have spent most of my time and energy—walking the spiritual path and exploring the spiritual dimension of my being. Through the years I have practiced meditation and *yoga*, read all the pertinent books on spirituality, and tried to keep my life as simple as possible—thus a cab driver. Of course, there have been many pitfalls along the way. Yes, there were times when I was spiritually lazy; yes, there were times when I wavered from the path; yes, there were times when I gave up altogether—yes, yes, yes, yes, and more yeses. But I still come back to it all the same. The spiritual path has been the one constant in my life; it's the only pursuit I have never totally given up on. Slowly but surely I creep along this glorious path, even though it appears at times I'm getting nowhere. And what intrigues me the most about being on the spiritual path is this notion of a Being called God, the Greatest Mystery in the universe.

God has always been a focal point in my life. One of my earliest recollections of God was when I was around six years old. I was watching TV and it was time for bed. But when the movie Barabbas came on, my parents thought it would be a good idea for me to stay up a little while longer and catch a portion of the flick. I didn't mind; I always enjoyed staying up past my bedtime.

In the beginning of the movie, Pontius Pilate came out of the Halls of Justice to address the masses. Soon afterward, Barabbas came out and walked to the left of Pilate; then Jesus came out and walked to the right. My eyes were transfixed on the lower, right hand side of the TV screen. I tried in vain to get a glimpse of this figure called Jesus Christ. I was at an age when I still believed in Santa Claus and the Easter Bunny, so when I finally saw the face of Jesus Christ, I wasn't seeing an actor playing Jesus Christ, I was seeing Jesus Christ Himself, the God Almighty. Unfortunately, when a commercial came I was sent to bed and the experience ended. But my journey into God had begun, and it continues to this day.

Why my interest in God began at such an early age is something only God can explain; why it continues is because God continually widens my eyes with moments like Barabbas. It's like He's been taking me by the hand and waiting for opportune moments to fill my soul with a little more of His never-ending Glory. From Barabbas to now, my soul has been touched by many a moment, giving me the strength and inspiration I need to continue my journey. I wish I could elaborate on all these moments in my life, but that would be a book in itself. There are, however, a few worth mentioning.

A few years after Barabbas, I became an altar boy. Not that I was a religious person; I was anything but. My main reason for becoming an altar boy was to get a day off from school at the end of the school year and go on the altar boy picnic. The altar boys were the select few who got the day off, while everyone else had to attend class. Memorizing Latin and getting up at 6:00 A. M. for early Mass seemed worth it to me.

I became an altar boy at St. Peter's Cathedral in Marquette, Michigan. It was an old church that was Victorian in style. It was also the residence of a Roman Catholic Bishop, and I even served Mass for him on occasion in his own private chapel.

St. Peter's was by far the finest piece of ecclesiastical architecture in all of northern Michigan. Its towering walls of stone rose majestically above the city landscape, and two golden belfries pierced the sky. In front were a dozen or so long steps that led up to   huge oak doors and elaborate marble columns, and exquisite stained glass windows lined both sides of the building. This edifice definitely had an imposing look to it, especially to a ten year old, and inside you could hear the echoes from the past, all the way back to Christ Himself, reverberating throughout its stone walls.

What fascinated me the most about being an altar boy at St. Peter's was not when I was serving Mass but when I was all alone inside its walls in the wee hours of the morning. The altar boys were always the first to arrive, and I was usually the first one there. (I wonder why? Was God already planning my destiny way back then?)

Nothing could compare to being alone inside that church during the early morning darkness. Those moments were moments I have rarely experienced anywhere else in my life. They were moments when I entered sacred time, to use Mircea Eliade's terminology. Today, some thirty five years later, the memories of those moments are still vivid in my mind.

As I walked up the steps to St. Peter's Cathedral in the pre-dawn morning and opened the huge oak doors, I immediately found myself in a realm of total darkness, disturbed only by a few flickers of candlelight. Slowly I moved through the nave, mesmerized by my surroundings. Soon the silence became thunderous, the darkness captivating, the candlelight soothing. Each step I took into the dark took me further away from the here and now. In no time at all I was transported from ordinary reality to sacred reality, taken to the foot of the altar of God, where I felt His Almighty Presence, where I felt His Power and Might. With devout reverence, I knelt before His crucified Body and gazed into His loving eyes through the flickering candlelight, wondering what kind of a being this Being called God was. No answers came, no revelations were revealed, but that was of little concern to a ten year old. Sharing this quiet moment with God was all that mattered, was all my young soul needed. It was the closest I ever felt to God while being inside a church, and it still holds true today. If I'm out walking at night and I come by a church and if the doors are still open, I'll step inside that sacred darkness and share a moment with God.

Of course, all good things must come to an end. These childhood moments of rapture faded into oblivion as quickly as they came, and as they faded I was brought back to ordinary reality, ready to begin my illustrious duties as a pious altar boy. First order of business...sipping the wine. So much for religious piety.

Years later while I was in high school, another strange occurrence happened. For reasons unknown, I picked myself up out of a chair, grabbed a pen and paper, went into my bedroom and started writing. What motivated me to do this I'm not completely sure; I was more in a hypnotic trance than anything else. I heard a voice inside me say, "Go write," and so I did.

What I wrote first was the date, Feb. 21, 1972. I figured if I ever make it as a writer, we can all know the day it actually started. This date hasn't meant anything yet, but there's still time; something, some force or being, made me date that day.

After writing a few poetic lines down, I went out and showed my mom. Within a couple of minutes there were tears in her eyes. I really didn't know what she was crying about because I really didn't know what I had just written. It must have sounded good, but I'm sure I didn't have a clue to what the meaning of my words were. All beginning writers probably can relate to this: something moves them and they start writing, not knowing for sure if what they're writing makes any sense at all. I don't know if what I wrote made any sense at all, but it sure had an effect on dear old mom, which might have been a sign from God. "Keep it up," He was saying through her tears, "there's hope for you yet."

My sudden desire to write was once again God's way of reaching into my soul and pulling it towards some unknown region. He wanted to introduce me to a world vastly different from the one in which I was living. Few people knew of its exact whereabouts, and God was doing His best to show me the way. The almighty pen became my transport, and God was my pilot.

This momentary writing spell completely changed the spiritual dynamics of my soul. Up till now, only outer forces were affecting its movement; now inner forces were. There I was, one moment playing happily and foolishly along the shoreline of being, not having a care in the world, when all of a sudden God started enticing me into the water. Without any hesitation whatsoever, without any fear or doubt, I stepped right into that water, ready for my new task at hand—writing. From what had just transpired, this little writing exercise probably had the equivalence of getting my toes wet—but hey, at least I got wet.

A couple years later when I went to college, I became an avid reader. Herman Hesse, Carl Jung, and Alan Watts became my new best friends. I shared many wonderful moments with these three guys; they taught me so much about the spiritual path and what the true meaning of God was. They made me begin to realize that God was an experiential journey, not someone to wait until death for.

After college not much happened to me until my mid thirties when I started a new kind of activity—hiking. Trekking through the wilderness and listening to the sounds of nature became my new passion in life, my new way of exploring my spirituality; nature's pathways became my new pathways to God. Hiking was such an exhilarating experience for me that it revitalized my spirit and brought renewed vigor back into my life. I felt like a kid again, happily playing in the playgrounds of nature. I enjoyed it so much out there that I continue hiking today, and probably will continue doing it for a long time to come.

Where I've been doing all of my hiking is in a place unparalleled anywhere else in the world. It's a place where time stops and the eternal speaks. It's a place your soul will forever long for, no matter how many times you go there. It's a place known as the American West, home to the heavyweights of nature.

I love the American West. It's a land of enchanting beauty and magical landscapes. From the radiant blue waters of Crater Lake to the breathtaking views of the Grand Canyon, from the colossal size of

Yosemite Valley to the blue-green lakes of Glacier National park, the West is filled with awesome shrines to the Divine.

Untouched by time, these magnificent masterpieces echo a past that is millions of years old; they remind you of a time when rock and water reigned supreme and we were merely a glimmer in nature's eyes. Walking across these timeless terrains, you can't help but be overcome by a sense of wonder. Their lofty appearance and powerful elegance awaken you to a higher reality; they make you feel part of a greater whole, an unbreakable whole, a whole in which all of being merges into one. Yes, the West is a wonderful place to be, inspiring all who step on it's hallowed ground.

Hiking these sacred places has been equaled only by my times alone inside St. Peter's Cathedral. The deep canyons and majestic mountains of the West have become my new cathedrals, their spires my new steeples. Once again I find myself in the presence of the Almighty, feeling His Power surge through my being. Whether it's a thundering Yosemite waterfall or a raging King's Canyon river, I hear His mighty Voice loud and clear; whether it's a quiet Yellowstone meadow or a crystalline-clear Glacier lake, I see the purity and beauty of His Spirit; whether it's an ageless Sequoia evergreen or an enduring Teton peak, I sense His permanent and everlasting Nature; whether it's the chasmal Grand Canyon depths or a massive Rocky Mountain mountain top, I feel the breadth and depth of His Being. He's everywhere out here, in everything, speaking to me, preaching to me, singing to me, teaching me the ways of the Spirit, imploring me to adhere to the Call of the Divine. No matter where I'm at, I cannot escape His pervasive Power. It surrounds me, penetrates me, extends through me and outward towards infinity...no, it's even more than that: it's a Power I'm meant to become—I am that Power! That's what these natural wonders are trying to tell me; their colorful rocks and sparkling clear waters are doorways to the Infinite, beacons of eternity, guiding me to the everlasting shores of Being. Yes, time will eat away at the rock; yes, time will muddy the waters; yes, time will turn these marvels to dust—but the Power that's behind them, the Power that emanates from them, the Power that creates and sustains them, will remain forever. That's who I am. That's my destiny. That's my future.

The wonders of nature are reflections of the Power within; they are outward manifestations of the unseen spirit—that's what the western wilderness has taught me. It has awakened me to a Power that's inside all of us, a Power that permeates all of being. The feelings we all share while standing in these environments—the feelings of awe and wonder—is our way of acknowledging this Power that flows through us: through our bodies, through the rock and water, through the whole universe itself. It's there for everyone to appreciate and enjoy; it discriminates against no one. And there are times when it can even become personal.

I recently had a personal encounter with Power in the Sky Lakes Wilderness just outside of Crater Lake National Park in Oregon. It was a mild encounter, a somewhat amusing encounter, but an encounter all the same.

As I began my hike, I was immediately startled by a huge crunching sound in the forest; it sounded like a giant log being slammed hard to the ground. Soon afterward, I heard what sounded like an animal running off into the distance. I rushed ahead to see what it was, but saw nothing. I was dumfounded by what had just happened. I couldn't

imagine any animal making such a loud noise; deer are too quiet, and a

bear would have to have fallen straight down from the tree tops to make

a sound as alarming as that. Shrugging my shoulders I moved onward,

but before I could get very far the scene before me completely changed.

An eerie silence started to settle in; not a sound could be heard and

there wasn't a breath of wind. Trees stood like quiet sentinels as I

peered deep into the wood. This idyllic setting was more like a still

painting: quiet, peaceful, motionless. Then suddenly a strange

sensation came over me, a sensation I have never felt in all my years of

hiking. I could feel a pair of eyes staring at me from behind the wood;

they weren't human eyes, or even animal eyes, but the eyes of some

other being. Were they the eyes of the creature I just heard a moment

ago? Who knows? All I knew is that these eyes, or rather this

presence, was all around me; I couldn't escape it, nor did I want to. I

was actually enjoying this experience; there was no fear in me, only an

eerie calm. "Who are you?" I asked, smiling. "I know you're out there,

but I don't know who you are"—or did I? As I stood there pondering this situation, something inside me told me the following: that presence out there is you in a higher state of awareness. As odd as that sounded, I wasn't taken aback by it. Instead, I accepted it fully, without hesitation, and this acceptance gave me an uncanny sense of freedom and joy. For I knew if this was the case, then there was nothing to be afraid of. Even if a hand reached out of the wood and took my life at that moment, I knew I could never be destroyed. Where I lived eternally was out there in those eyes, not here inside this body. Coming to this realization, I realized there was nothing to fear—ever! I would always be part of this presence—that gigantic Eye of God observing all. My feelings were all but verified when I saw another hiker coming from the other direction; he was like a messenger sent from God.

We stopped and talked a bit, then he said something that completely astounded me. He said: "You know, I was going to do some backpacking out here, but this place just doesn't feel right. There's something strange going on out here and I'm leaving." We said our good-byes and went our separate ways, but I was cracking up inside. I couldn't believe what I had just heard. He was having the exact same experience as I was but had a completely different reaction to it: he was running away from it, while I was running right into the teeth of it. But isn't that the way Power is: some people fear it, while others crave it. There isn't anything good or evil about Power; it's just Power, and everyone reacts differently to it. Why do some people love thunder and lightning, while others hate it? Why are some people attracted to powerful people, while others shy away? It all has to do with Power. Take, for instance, a master in the martial arts. He is someone who should be admired, but not necessarily someone to be afraid of. Granted, he can perform incredible feats of power and strength, but that's no reason to fear the guy. All he is doing is demonstrating the Power that exists inside all of us; he is showing us our true potential. Never is his intention to harm. Still, there are those who shy away from him; they are too intimidated by his presence to see what they truly can become—they don't see the eyes in the wilderness, only their fearful little bodies. Others, though, are fearless. They go right up to him and say, "Teach me. I want to learn." That day I chose to run with the Master.

I would like to make one other point about hiking before I continue. Nothing is more symbolic about the spiritual journey than a hike to the top of a mountain. I have hiked several peaks, Mt. Elbert in Colorado and Wheeler Peak in both New Mexico and Nevada to name a few, and they are always painstaking experiences. The trails are usually long and arduous, and it seems to take forever to get to the top. The closer you get, the more difficult the hike becomes. You're up over 13,000 ft. and you begin to experience shortness of breath. Your thighs ache and burn with each step you take, and you wonder if you're ever going to make it. "Where is it," you plead, "Where is it? How much farther do I have to go—where's the damn summit!" And before you know it, there you are, standing on top of a mountain, witnessing the greatest sight your eyes have ever seen, the pain and agony of a moment ago a distant memory.

And isn't that how the spiritual journey is. It's a long and difficult path, and the closer you get to the pearly-gates, the greater the challenges become; the biggest tests are yet to be met. You are going to have to rely on all your spiritual experience and discipline to guide you through the entranceway, but once you enter, it will be the greatest experience you will ever have, the pain and agony of the long journey gone forever, vanishing into a sea of eternal bliss. That's what awaits us all, and that's the journey this book is going to take.

So where has this journey taken me to? In what exotic land do I now find myself standing in? I believe I'm standing in a place few people have ever stood. I feel like I'm atop a huge precipice, looking out over a vast horizon and staring into the sea of eternity. For I believe this journey has taken me to the edge of infinity, where I have been given a glimpse of the most beautiful idea in all creation. What a philosopher's dream: to witness the greatest idea of all. Now I am in no way so presumptuous as to claim ownership of this idea; this idea has been around forever; it's just that my brain cells have been able to tune in to its frequency. And what I have been able to tune into has enabled me to accomplish something that I never thought possible. And what is that, you ask? To put it simply, it is this: I believe I have proven beyond the shadow of a doubt the existence of God. What! You, a cab driver—a nobody!—proving the existence of God! Who the hell do you think you are! The greatest minds in human history have never been able to prove successfully the existence of God, so what makes you so special? You must be one incredibly arrogant son of a....

I can hear these complaints already, and you know, they might be right. It's quite possible that I'm a complete ignoramus who doesn't have a clue what he's talking about. If that's the case, then this book will never see the light of day, and the only one who will ever know about it will be me, myself, and I. On the other hand, it might be the case that this idea of mine does make sense, and in no way whatsoever can it ever be proven wrong. I might have actually entered a cryptic realm where spiritual secrets are revealed. Things like that happen on the spiritual path. Has it happened to me? It's too soon to tell. All I know for sure is that I am at a point in my life where I have no choice but to write this book. What happens after this is beyond my control. All I can do is write it and let the chips fall where they may. At worst, writing this book might be nothing more than a spiritual exercise between me and God. Once it's finished, it's destined for dust in the closet. At best, this book might catch a publisher's eye and find its way into the public domain for all to see and read. Only time will tell which path this book takes. But if this book ever does find you, it won't be because of my doing, it will be because of what this book is all about—it will be God's doing.

I know it sounds a bit strange that a cab driver is claiming to have proven the existence of God. No need to fret yet; I still might be crazy. But before you send in the men in the white coats, you should hear what I have to say; I might surprise you. Seriously though, who I am and what I do for a living shouldn't in itself discredit me from speaking on spiritual matters. Granted, I'm not a Ph.D., M.D., or the most prominent person in society, but why should that matter anyway? Who you are rarely matters when it comes to the inner kingdom. The spiritual path is filled with all kinds of lowly types who have achieved greatness. Was it not a carpenter's helper who started Christianity? Was it not a prince-turned-beggar who started Buddhism? Was it not an illiterate man who started Islam? These three men—Jesus, Buddha and Mohammed—were not towering figures of their day, yet they founded three of the greatest religions known to man. Now I am in no way trying to equate myself with these three individuals; far from it. All I'm trying to show you is that a simple existence can lead to extraordinary accomplishments. If a carpenter's helper can do it, if a beggar can do it, if a man who can't even read or write can do it, then why not a cab driver? Such is the way of the spiritual path.

When it comes right down to it, God probably prefers it this way. If someone is extremely rich, or if someone is extremely intelligent, then we all stand in awe of such a person and believe we cannot do what he or she can do. However, if someone of simple means does something great, then we've found someone we can relate to, someone we can call our equal. We can then find ourselves saying, "Well, if he can do it, then so can I." This is what God wants. He wants us all to realize we can all do something special. There's no reason to feel that only the rich and powerful or the brightest people on the planet can do great things. We all can. All it takes is a commitment to God and everything else will be taken care of, even greatness and success.

But even if it turns out that greatness never comes our way, and even if success eludes us our whole lives, we who walk the path will never feel short-changed or harbor any ill-feelings towards a society who discounts our value merely on the basis of our outward status. The reason for such benevolence is based primarily on the fact that we have a different value system than most. We measure our success not by outer wealth but by inner growth. As long as our internal barometer indicates we're heading in the right direction, we feel no need to apologize or be embarrassed by our outer circumstances. We are God-seekers, and we make the necessary sacrifices to follow our dream.

Why do you think it's the case that all the saints throughout history have led simple, humble lives? Why do you think so many people dedicated to the spiritual path flock to monasteries? Why do you think certain mystics and *yogis* become hermits? The reason is obvious: it frees them from the demands of the outer world so that they can pursue God on a full time basis. If you want to go a long way on the spiritual path, it's going to take as much time and effort as any other endeavor in life does. Do you think an athlete can become an Olympic star if he works out on Saturday afternoons only? Do you think an employee of a major corporation can become its CEO if he works only part time? Of course not. So why should it be any different for someone on the spiritual path? That's why it's so insulting to me when I hear someone say, "O it's so nice that you're into your spirituality, but don't you want to get a real job?"

This is what has always been the problem when it comes to our spirituality: how do you pursue God in a material world? If you are working twenty hours a day at your career, or if you are always worrying about your money, how can you ever make time for God? And if you can't make time for God, how can God make time for you? "Yeah, right, I'll do it tomorrow." But tomorrow never comes, and before you know it you're at the end of your life and you realize you are no closer to God than you were at the beginning of your life. On the other hand, if you want to pursue a spiritual life, how do you survive in the material world? If joining a monastery or a religious organization isn't to your liking, and you don't want to become a hermit, what are you to do, where are you to go? You have to eke out an existence somehow, and whatever existence you eke out, it has to be one that creates the least amount of disruption to your spiritual life; otherwise you will be going nowhere fast.

So what is one to do? How does one find a way out of this dilemma? How does one find a balance between survival and spiritual growth? Unfortunately, there is no easy answer here; there are probably as many answers as there are people walking the path. You and you alone are going to have to be the ultimate decision maker; no one else can do it for you. Whatever you decide to do, though, you better make sure it gives you as much freedom as possible to pursue your spiritual goals. To make this happen, you are going to have to know what your interests are, what your psychical make-up is, and what disturbs you the least. If you can figure all this out, then hopefully you will find a niche in this world that allows you to survive and pursue God at the same time.

Luckily for me, I have been able to find answers to the questions above. As I mentioned earlier, I studied philosophy in college. This means I enjoy exploring and analyzing ideas; in a word, I'm a thinker. From this we can make the following observation about myself: my area of interest is the realm of thought, and my psychical make-up is that of a thinker and a loner, since thinkers like to be alone when they think. This is quite telling about my spirituality. What it tells me is that exploring thought is my way of walking the path; thought is my vehicle, my pathway, to God. Now all that's left is for me to find an activity in life that will disturb my walk on the path the least; and that activity is none other than—driving. So there you have it in a nutshell: my interest is thought, my psychical make-up is that of a thinker and a loner, and what disturbs me the least is driving. This is how a forged a spiritual path.

Before I say anything more, I want to make it perfectly clear that I'm not trying to say that only people like me our spiritual. That's not the case at all. Most people want to fall in love, get married, raise a family, and hopefully find a career they can appreciate and enjoy. There is nothing wrong with that, and they can still lead very spiritually fulfilling lives. What I'm talking about is that there are a few of us who want to go further down the path; we want to head out towards the outer perimeter where very few humans have walked. Call it seeking the

White Light, becoming one with the universe, one with God, or whatever you want to call it, but we want to be able to explore the spiritual depths of our being so that we can expand our spiritual awareness. To do this we need to let go of excess baggage; material possessions and concerns can be more of a burden than a help. We need to lighten the load if we want to make it to the outer fringes of being, and if someone is fortunate enough to make it to the end, don't be surprised if you see him in nothing more than a loincloth and sandals.

Now back to me.

As I just stated, exploring thoughts is my way of walking the path. This all makes perfect sense to me now, but for years it never did. While I was spending my time driving through life, I thought I was wasting my life away, living a meaningless, purposeless existence. "What am I suppose to do with my life?" I would always say to myself, but no answer ever came to me. So all I did was keep driving and work on my spiritual development, hoping something better would eventually come my way. But it never did. And now I can happily say, "Thank God for that."

The reason I now feel this way is because I have been given the greatest gift a thinker could ever possibly get—proving the existence of God. There is no idea greater than this one in all eternity, and here it is living inside my mind. Sometimes it pays to go a little further down the road.

Now the question could arise as to whether or not this could have happened to me if I had a career and was making lots of money. It's possible, but I seriously doubt it. The pressures and responsibilities of my life would have been too great, the stress too overwhelming. How could I ever have heard my inner voice speaking to me; the static in my life would have drowned out any sounds coming from the deeper realms. No, I couldn't have taken that path. My spiritual growth would have been thwarted, and my life would have become empty and meaningless.

Instead, I needed to find a lifestyle that was more conducive to my personality. If my thoughts were going to have any chance of developing and growing, they were going to need as little interference as possible from the outside world. My mind needed to become like a pool of water on a windless day: clear and calm, without any ripples. If ripples appeared, then my thoughts would become discombobulated and I would be thrown off course; the bigger the ripples, the further off course I'd get.

Driving was the perfect solution; it kept the ripples to a minimum. My thoughts were given the freedom to roam wherever they wanted to, taking me to places I never knew existed. My mind became like a raging torrent, free and vibrant, boiling with fervid effervescence, rapidly flowing to the outer reaches of being, where all things are possible, even proving the existence of God. Driving was key in all this, and it gave me the peace and serenity I so desperately needed. As I drove down city streets and country roads, I cruised through my fields of thought—and cruised I did, all the way to the doorsteps of God, where He said: "You found me. Now let the rest of the world know."

This was an extraordinary event for me. In an instant I saw into the true nature of God. Call it a mystical flash, a lucid moment, or intuitive insight, but in one brief moment I saw the philosophy I've been seeking my whole life unfold before my mind's eye; it was like all the pieces of a puzzle coming together at once. I saw how it all works and what it all means; I saw how this universe has purpose and meaning and that we are all key players in guiding it to its ultimate destiny; I saw how all life matters, even with all its pain and anguish and sorrow. It was quite an event, an awe-inspiring one, one that changed my life forever.

What I did to cause this spiritual revelation was this: I stepped out of this universe and into eternity. Now I'm not saying I had a mystical experience; what I am saying is that it had to do with my area of expertise: it was a thought experiment. I wondered what went on for all eternity before this universe came into being, and what will go on for all eternity after this universe ceases to exist. After contemplating this, I came to one obvious conclusion: there's a forever going on out there, and it's been going on forever. This universe is nothing more than a nexus point between an infinite past and an infinite future. So, for example, if nothing existed before this universe, and if nothing is going to exist after this universe, then that's our forever: an eternity of non-existence, where for one brief moment existence appeared. Maybe there have been other brief periods of existence throughout eternity. Maybe not. Maybe there's been an existence that's lasted forever. At this point we just don't know. Whatever it is, though, it adds up to forever.

What I intend to do in this book is fill up this forever for you, and I believe you'll have to come to the same conclusion as I did. I believe you'll find that there is only one thing that's been happening forever, and one thing only—and that is, God's been happening, and God alone.

So there you have it. That's what this book is going to be about. Are you intrigued yet? Are you ready to read on? After all, I'm just a cab driver.

CHAPTER 2

INFINITE BEING

Where do I begin? How do I start this impossible task of proving the existence of God? Some people think I'm a fool for even trying. "Don't you know His Existence can never be proved," they say. "He's supposed to be accepted on faith, and faith alone." Well, one thing for sure is, if He exists He can do whatever He wants because He's God. If He wants His Existence proved, then so be it. What I don't understand is why me? Believe me, if I'm able to pull this off, I'll be just as shocked as you are as to why I was the chosen one.

To start things out, I think it's only appropriate to define what God is. From what the great religions of the world tell us, God is basically this: He is an Infinite Being who is Omnipotent, Omniscient, Omnipresent and the Source of all creation. I don't believe an atheist would have a problem with this definition; his only problem is that this Being exists at all.

The key word in the definition of God is the word infinite. The fact that God is infinite is what makes Him so intriguing. There is nothing more incomprehensible in all of eternity than an Infinite Being. Trying to fathom His Existence is like trying to put an ocean into a glass jar; it just can't be done. No matter how hard we try, we will always be off by an infinite amount. That being said, we are still able to learn a few facts about an Infinite Being.

First, He is boundless, limitless; He stretches from one end of eternity to the other, embracing all that exists. Nothing exists outside of

Him—nothing. Second, He has no beginning or end; He always was, always is, and always will be, forever and ever. And third, and this is the most important point of all, there can be only one. To say otherwise is absurd. If you're saying there's an infinite being A and an infinite being B, what are you saying? You're saying there's a boundary between two infinite beings: infinite being A lacks what infinite being B has, and infinite being B lacks what infinite being A has. Since these two infinite beings lack what the other has, they both become bounded and limited and thus cannot be truly infinite. Remember, and Infinite Being cannot have any boundaries or limits whatsoever.

A simple aphorism can best explain how there can be only one Infinite Being. It goes as follows: 'There can be only one One; more than one means two; two means boundaries; boundaries means limits; limits means finite; thus no Infinite Being.' If an Infinite Being exists, then He has no equal; He is the One and only; He is the Infinite One; He is the God in which we seek.

If I might divert off topic for a moment, this is the problem religions have been having forever. They all claim to have the one true God, but there can be only one Infinite Being. All these different Gods are really

one and the same God. There is no difference between Yahweh and

Allah, or any other God; they are just different names of the Nameless

One. To say otherwise means Yahweh is not part of Allah, and Allah is

not part of Yahweh, which means a boundary has been drawn between

Yahweh and Allah, making them both limited and thus finite. If

religions claim to worship an Infinite Being, as they all claim to do,

then they are all worshipping the same Being, the same God.

Hopefully, religions will come to their senses someday and realize this,

then they can stop playing this foolish game of "My Daddy is better

than your Daddy." Instead, they can learn to appreciate and respect the

religious diversity and heritage of the human race and look upon all

religions as great works of art sent down from the Divine. We can only

hope.

One more point needs to be made about religion before we continue.

Since there can be only one Infinite Being, all religions are nothing

more than different denominations of the One Great Religion

worshipping God. If a certain denomination suits you, join it; if not, do what others do and start your own; if that doesn't suit you, do what I do—go it alone. God is there, whichever road you take. He doesn't care which faith you belong to, only that you have faith in Him. Enough said.

Getting back to my main topic, all I have to do is prove the existence of an Infinite Being and I've proven the existence of God because only God can be infinite. So how do I go about proving the existence of an Infinite Being? The old ways never seem to work. We try to show a Creator exists by showing that there is law and order in the universe, or we look at the beauty and intricacy of nature and conclude there has to be a cosmic Interior Decorator designing it all: just look at the complexity of a snowflake and you know there has to be a Divine Intelligence out there somewhere. But all the atheist has to do is sit back in his easy chair, sip a cool one, and say, "Just chance, just luck; the odds have to kick in sooner or later. If you put a monkey in front of a typewriter long enough, he'll eventually type out the Bible. That doesn't mean there's any meaning or purpose behind it." And so the battle rages on: two beliefs in eternal conflict forever and ever.

But beliefs come and go. Our history is filled with all kinds of beliefs that have either died a slow death or become fact. Was there not a time in our past when we believed the earth was flat? If we walked in a straight line, we thought we would eventually fall off the face of the earth. Are there any 'flatlanders' today? Does anyone actually believe the earth is flat? Of course not. It's a belief that no longer exists. Up until recently, about 400 years ago, the Catholic Church believed we were the center of the universe; they thought the whole cosmos revolved around our little old planet. Then a quiet Italian by the name of Galileo proved the earth was not the center of the universe; it was just an insignificant planet revolving around an insignificant star in an insignificant galaxy. The Church was outraged by such a notion. It screamed heresy and put Galileo under house arrest for the rest of his life. I'm sure there were 'higher-ups' at the Vatican who went to their graves still believing our planet was the center of the universe. Does anyone believe that today? Of course not. It's just another belief that bit the dust.

That's what I intend to do with atheism. I want to crush it out of existence; I want to efface it off the face of the earth; I want to make it a philosophy of the past; I want to hear the children of the future say, "Remember when there used to be atheists." To accomplish this, I have come up with a novel idea. I am going to boldly go where no man has gone before. I am going to take my rarefied sword, jump into the fiery pit and slay the dragon once and for all: I'm going to prove Infinity itself. A huge task indeed, but one that can be done with relative ease, if you don't mind me saying.

CHAPTER 3

INFINITY

What is Infinity? Before we delve into that, it should be noted that Infinity is even more bizarre than Infinite Being because Infinity includes Infinite Being. I know I must have just completely confused the hell out of you, but hang in there, it'll all make sense in due time. For now, just trust in Infinity's Logic and leave the rest to me.

The best way to explain Infinity is with an analogy using math and numbers. When it comes to math, we can create infinite sets of infinities. We can create an infinite set of positive numbers, negative

numbers, even numbers, odd numbers, fractions, fractions between 0

and 1, between 1 and 2, and so on and so on, *ad infinitum*. All these so-

called infinities, though, are ultimately limited because each set lacks

what the other sets have. For example, an infinite set of positive

numbers lack what an infinite set of negative numbers have, and vice

versa. Since both sets lack what the other has, neither set can claim

infinite status. Like it is with Infinite Being, if a boundary exists, then

no one set can be the one true infinity.

In the universe of numbers, there can be only one true infinity, and

that infinity is one in which all numbers are included: all positive

numbers, all negative numbers, all fractions, all decimals, and any other

number that might exist. There can be no infinity equal to or greater

than this one because this infinity includes all the numbers in existence;

nothing more could possibly exist, and anything less is just that—less

than infinity. All those other infinite sets of infinities are at best

pseudo-infinities; they ultimately serve no purpose and prove nothing

here. If we want to find God, we need to find an Infinity like the one that includes all numbers. If we find this Infinity, then we've found the place where God resides. Is He home?

Now, what is the best way to describe this Infinity when it comes to being? The best way, I believe, is as follows: this Infinity is an Infinity where existence exists forever and is sustained by an Infinite Being. No other infinity can top this one. Since this Infinity includes an Infinite Being, and since there is no being greater than an Infinite Being, there can be no infinity greater than this one. If I can prove this Infinity exists, then we've found God. If I prove anything less, Infinity collapses and God is crushed out of existence. The atheist can then jump for joy and sing his victory song from sea to shining sea. But if I can prove an eternity filled with existence, if I can prove being and Infinite Being existing forever in perfect harmony, then we have found our one true Infinity. Nothing more could possibly exist, and everything that can exist, does; Infinity's Inn will be booked forever. This is the only Infinity that matters, the only one that counts, the only one that's boundless, the only one that God can exist in. Anything less than this would be equivalent to an infinite set of positive numbers; it will never add up to Infinity. God needs all numbers if He is to Be. If He is short just one number, He is that much short of Infinity; thus neither He nor Infinity can exist. All must exist if He is to exist. Such is the way of God.

Now that we know the Infinity we're looking for, we can begin the process of trying to prove Its existence. To start things out, I have come up with an equation that will take us right into Infinity. It goes as follows:

$$\text{Infinity of Being} + \text{Infinite Being} = \text{Infinity}.$$

I know this equation sounds pretty impressive, but believe me, this is no $E = mc^2$ equation. All I'm trying to say is this: all of God's creation, plus God Himself, equals our one true Infinity; or, if you prefer, the created aspect of God, plus the uncreated aspect of God, equals the totality of God. Remember, God just doesn't embody all of existence; He embodies all of Himself—Infinite Being. If He didn't, then boundaries would emerge and we can kiss our Infinity good-bye. We need an eternity of existence enveloped by an Infinite Being to get our

Infinity, and that's what this equation does—it opens the door to Infinity.

Now, how do we break into this equation? We can't start with Infinite Being because that's what we're trying to prove. We can't start with Infinity because we need an Infinite Being first before we can have Infinity. So what's left? An Infinity of Being—ah, that's the ticket, that's the way into this equation. Let's enter here and see where it takes us.

CHAPTER 4

WAS THERE A FIRST UNIVERSE?

They say this universe of ours is around 15 billion years old, give or take a few billion years. They also say this universe is quite large, billions and billions of light years across. As impressive as all this sounds, it is of little interest to me here. My concern is not with the size or age of this universe or anything else that pertains to this universe. My concern goes beyond this universe; my concern is with what went on before this universe ever came into being. Was there another universe before this one, and if so, how many? Was there one, ten, a hundred, a thousand, a million, a billion, a billion trillion, a trillion zillion...?

Excluding infinity for the moment, whatever number we choose will be a finite number; therefore, there has to be a first universe, *i.e.* a beginning. So for the sake of argument, let's say our universe is the first universe that ever came into being.

If our universe is the first universe, then the atheist has only two ways to explain its appearance: either it came from something—existence, or it came from nothing—non-existence. Let's explore both options and see where they take us.

If the atheist says that our universe, the first universe, the first time existence ever came into being, came from nothing, then he's saying there was an infinite past when only nothing existed; there was blank, nada, a forever of nothingness before our universe appeared. Question. How long does it take forever to come to an end? It takes forever, does it not? In other words, forever can never come to an end. If that's the case, then our universe could never come into being because it would have to wait for forever to come to an end, and that can never happen. Therefore, a first universe could never emerge out of nothing.

There's another problem for the atheist if he believes that nothing existed forever before our universe came into being. If something exists forever, then it exists forever: it always was, always is, and always will be forever and ever. It can never come to an end. Once our universe appeared, nothing ceased to exist because existence negates non-existence. Both cannot exist at the same time; either we have existence or non-existence, but not both. Since we now have existence, non-existence no longer exists. Question. How can something that has existed forever, all of a sudden cease to exist? It can't. It can never happen. For nothing to exist forever, there can never be a first universe. Therefore, nothing can never be responsible for a first universe. It can only be responsible for nothing—literally.

The only option left for the atheist is to say our universe came from something, that is, some form of existence. Right from the get-go we know this theory is dead in the water, because before our universe came into being, there was no existence of any kind to speak of; existence did not appear until our first universe appeared. So how can we speak of existence before that point? We can't. Therefore, there can be no Thing that starts a first universe.

But let's not be so hard on the atheist. Let's give him the benefit of the doubt and say there was this primordial Thing that existed before our universe came into being. Like nothing, this Thing had to exist forever first, and then one day in eternity it decided to shapeshift into a universe. No matter how you cut it, shape it, or slice it, this primordial Thing could never accomplish such a feat because it would run into the same problem as the 'nothing theory' does. Since it takes forever for forever to come to an end, this Thing could never shapeshift into anything, much less a universe. It would have to remain a Thing, and only a Thing, forevermore. Therefore, this primordial Thing could never be responsible for a first universe.

So what's an atheist to do? Where does he go from here? He can't bring God into the equation because he doesn't believe in God. So what's left? If nothing can't produce a first universe, if some thing can't produce a first universe, and if God can't be allowed into the mix, then how does an atheist find a way out of this first universe dilemma?

If you don't mind, my dear atheist, I might have a way out for you, and it doesn't even involve God. "What is it?" he asks in desperation. It's simply this: who says there has to be a first universe? Maybe there never was a first universe to begin with. "What does that mean?" asks the atheist. Well, if there isn't a first universe, that means there isn't a finite number of universes, which means the only alternative is what...infinite universes. The first universe problem solved.

The atheist pauses for a moment and contemplates my idea. Then he says, "Instead of one universe that is cold, dark, empty, and meaningless, there are infinite universes that are cold, dark, empty, and meaningless." He pauses again, thinking about this theory, and then his eyes light up. "I like it," he says, grinning. "Why should I care how many universes there are. As long as God isn't introduced into the mix, what difference does it make? We will still have a cold, dark, gloomy end—I love it! Go ahead, let there be infinite universes."

What the atheist doesn't realize is that by acknowledging infinite universes he has just lost the argument; it is game, set, match, and he's standing on the losing end of the court. Adios, amigo, you're history. Atheism is dead, and the God-seekers are victorious.

Of course, the atheist doesn't see it this way. He doesn't understand why acknowledging infinite universes is the same as acknowledging God, and I'm sure you don't understand it either. If I ended the book now, the atheist would never admit defeat, and you would never by my book. So I must continue onward so that I can show to one and all why infinite universes and God are one and the same.

CHAPTER 5

INFINITE UNIVERSES

To say there are infinite universes means there has been an eternity of existence; universes have been coming and going forever and ever; there has been no beginning to this process, and there is no end to this process. If this is the case (and if it isn't, then prove a first universe to me), then all that's left is to find the source of all these universes. Again, the atheist has only two choices: either they came from something or nothing.

We can dispatch immediately the theory of nothing as being responsible for infinite universes. Since existence has been around forever via infinite universes, there has never been a point in all eternity when non-existence existed—it never was! Therefore, nothingness could never be the source of infinite universes. Case closed.

The point I've just made reminds me of the phrase 'nature abhors a vacuum'. Scientists can find no place in the universe where pure emptiness, pure nothingness, exists. Every centimeter of space, every nook and cranny, is filled with sub-atomic particles or radiation of some kind. It seems our universe is a symbolic representation of eternity as a whole: nowhere is nothingness to be found.

What's left for the atheist is to say that some thing, some form of existence, is responsible for infinite universes. Before we rip this theory apart, we need to first examine what a thing is.

First, we know a thing has dimension; that is, it has shape, size, form, and in most cases weight (a neutrino is an example of a thing that is weightless). We also know that a thing has a beginning and an end.

This applies to space as well as to time. Look at me, for example. I am 5ft. 11in. tall, and I was born April 6, 1955. This means that my body (a thing) begins at one point in space and ends at another point in space. It also means that my body began to exist April 6, 1955, and it will end somewhere in the future. This is what I mean by a thing having a beginning and end in space as well as in time.

From this we can determine the following about a thing: it has boundaries, limits; in a word, it's finite. Question. How can something that is finite be responsible for something that is infinite? It can't. A thing will eventually run out of gas and there will still be infinite miles yet to go.

Now a physicist might ask, "What about energy? It has no shape, size, or form, but it still exists. True, but that doesn't mean energy has its own separate existence existing independently from this universe; it is still dependent on some form of existence, *i.e.* a thing. Take nuclear energy, for example. It might not have any shape, size, or form to it, but it is still dependent on the nucleus of the atom for its existence. Take away the nucleus and you take away the energy.

What this all means is that matter and energy are mutually dependent on each other for their own existence. It also means they're interchangeable: matter can become energy and energy matter. They are one and the same like water and ice, and if one ceases to exist, then so does the other. This is what $E = mc^2$ is all about: matter can be converted into energy and energy into matter, but if you take one or the other out of the equation, you take the other one out also. Thus neither one exists. Both are needed if both are to survive. Therefore, energy can never be independent and infinite on its own; it will always be dependent on the existence in which it is a part of for its own existence. Take away the existence and you take away the energy. Seeing energy in this light, we know it can never be the source of infinite universes. Wherever things come from, energy comes from the same place.

I would like to make a secondary point about a thing before we continue. It's not that important of a point, but one that I think needs to be made. It's not mandatory for a thing to be physical. It's only in our existential arrogance that we believe physical reality is the only game in town. It's quite possible that non-physical realities exist as well. There might be realities where astral beings, ghosts, angels, and even higher spiritual beings exist. But even if that's the case, these beings are still trapped by the same boundaries as we are. Like us, they have a shape, size, and form to their being; they also have a beginning and end to their existence, and thus are limited in scope. Therefore, they are finite, just like us. They too will cease to exist at some point in eternity. What will become of them? Where will they go? I can't give you the answer to that yet, but wherever their final resting place will be, will be ours also. We are all made of the same stuff—eventually.

With that said, I believe I have just shown how absurd it is for a thing to be the source of infinite universes, but I don't want to claim victory yet. I want to be fair, so I am going to explore this 'thing theory' in more detail so that the atheist can have ample opportunity to try to prove his point of view. To help him out, I am going to give him as much leeway as possible; I am going to throw him all the rope he wants so that he can try to save himself from falling into the abysmal depths. What he decides to with the rope in the end is totally up to him.

(What's the name of that game again, you know, the game where a man is dangling from the rope...O yea, that's right, Hang Man.)

The next problem for the atheist in dealing with the 'thing theory' is the *ad infinitum* argument. The *ad infinitum* argument goes as follows: thing A comes from thing B, thing B comes from thing C, thing C comes from thing D, and so on and so on, *ad infinitum*. In other words, we will never be able to get to the source of all things, because the thing we claim to be the source will always be preceded by another thing. Therefore, a thing can never be the source of anything. We will always be stuck with the question, "Where did that thing come from?"

"Wait a second," the atheist fires back, "just because we haven't found this most basic element doesn't mean it doesn't exist. It might very well be the case that it does exist; we just haven't found it yet."

Alright, I'll bite. Like I said, I'll give him as much leeway as possible.

So let's say we've found this most basic element in all eternity; all of existence is made up of this substance, and we will call this substance particle A.

Now if the atheist is saying that all infinite universes emerge out of particle A, then he's saying particle A stretches from one end of eternity to the other, making it infinite in size. We've already determined that only one Being can be infinite, and that Being is God. So if the atheist claims particle A is infinite, then all he's really doing is claiming the existence of God—my God! Our atheist has found the God Particle! I don't think he wants to go there. Changing the name from God to particle A will do absolutely nothing for the atheist; all it will do is give God a new name. As the old saying goes, a rose by any other name is still a....

"No, no, no," says the atheist. "It's not that particle A is infinite; rather, there are infinite particle A's, and since there are an infinite amount, they've always been around."

Okay. So instead of having one particle A that's infinite, we have infinite particle A's. Using this approach will cause nothing but problems for the atheist, problems that could end his career once and for all.

It might be the case that infinite universes are made up of infinite particle A's, but who says that's all there is to Infinity. It's quite possible that there is a particle B out there, creating its own set of infinite universes. Now we have two sets of infinite universes, both sets being mutually exclusive from each other. Now let's multiply this by infinity. Let's say there are infinite different particles out there, each particle creating its own set of infinite universes. Now we have infinite sets of infinite universes, each set being mutually exclusive from all the others. If particle A cannot be the source of two sets of infinite universes, how much less so can it be the source of infinite sets of infinite universes? As I said before, the only set that matters is the one that includes all of Infinity.

Now if this is too much for the atheist to comprehend, then let's say there are infinite universes made up of infinite particle A's, and let's say that's all there is to Infinity; nothing more exists, or will exist, in all eternity. If that's the case, then we have no choice but to go back to particle A and see it for what it is—a finite being.

Since there is more than one particle A, an infinite amount to be exact, we can safely assume that each particle A has its own separate existence, its own boundary, and is thus finite. Being finite, all particle A's must have a beginning and an end to their existence; at some point in eternity they will cease to exist. Where will they go? They can't dissolve into nothingness because nothingness doesn't exist in the 'infinite universes' scenario; they can't be reduced to anything less because they are the most elemental form of existence in all eternity. So what happens to them? Any ideas, my dear atheist?

The atheist thinks about this for a moment, then he comes up with a whole new game plan: he tries to abandon the 'infinite universes' theory altogether. He says, "Maybe our universe is the only universe, and what's unique about our universe is that it might have had a beginning, but it will expand forever. If it expands forever, then isn't our forever problem solved? We will have a universe that lasts forever, but there will be no ultimate meaning behind it; rather, it will be an existence that is cold, dark, and empty, and it will live on forevermore."

Nonsense, pure nonsense. All things, whether they are as small as an atom or as large as a universe, will have a beginning and an end to their existence. Our universe had a beginning; therefore, it will have an end. Only a Being that has no beginning has no end; everything else will disappear along the way.

What we have here is the 'first universe' problem all over again. There was an infinite past when this universe didn't exist. How could something that didn't exist forever all of a sudden exist forever? It doesn't make any sense whatsoever; it's total absurdity and turns Infinity's Logic right on its head. The only possible explanation is that universes have been blinking in and out of existence forever and ever. Our universe is one universe in a succession of infinite universes that come from an infinite past and will continue into an infinite future. There can be no other way.

The atheist is now completely dumfounded. He doesn't know what to do. In an act of desperation he comes up with one final theory. "Alright," he says, "so maybe this universe doesn't expand forever. Maybe it expands to a certain point, then it shrinks to a certain point, and this is what's been going on for all eternity: one big universe breathing in and out forever and ever. Our infinite past is covered, and our infinite future is covered. What do you think about that?"

Nice try, my friend, but this will get you absolutely nowhere. This is a different scenario, but it will yield the same old result.

What the atheist is referring to here is the oscillating theory of the universe. This is the theory where the universe expands to a certain point, and then gravity pulls it back in on itself, causing it to collapse to a miniscule point, where the process starts all over again. The only change the atheist makes is that this process has been going on forever. If this is the case, then we have to analyze what happens during the collapse.

Once the universe begins to collapse, galaxies will start crashing into each other, eventually crushing themselves out of existence. All that will remain will be atoms, and they too will be crushed out of existence. All that will be left will be sub-atomic particles (particle A's), and what will become of them? Eventually, they will have to be crushed into something that's been around forever because this universe has been around forever, and we all know by now there's only one Being that can hang around forever—Infinite Being. So eventually this universe will have to collapse into an infinite state of being. And since this universe will dissolve back into Infinite Being, it will no longer exist; only Infinite Being will exist at that point and nothing more. And when another universe appears on the horizon and starts to expand, it will be a brand-new universe because it will be emerging out of Infinite Being, not itself. And since this has been going on forever, our 'infinite universes' theory still holds. Like I said, different scenario, same old result. You are always going to run into this problem, my dear atheist, when you deal with forever.

If we could go back to the 'expanding universe' theory for a moment, we will have to conclude that this universe will have the same end as the oscillating universe. If this universe keeps expanding towards 'Foreverville,' as the atheist insists, then it must eventually expand into Infinite Being because that's the only Being that hangs around forever. Once there, our lovely universe will go bye-bye, making room for other universes to come and go as they please. So if the atheist insists that the expanding or oscillating universe goes on forever, then he runs the risk of heading towards a destiny he so desperately despises—Infinite Being.

In the long run, both these theories could be detrimental to an atheist's well-being; in fact, they might even put the fear of...into him. Think about it for a moment. Some day in the distant future, whether we are looking through a telescope at the largest parts of existence or through a microscope at the smallest parts of existence, we might come across a pair of Eyes looking at us—and who might that be? To the atheist, it might be the look that kills or the look that redeems. It's going to have to be up to him which look he chooses.

In this chapter I believe we have explored all possible options for the atheist. We have been fair, and we have been patient, but there seems to be no way out for the atheist. Neither thing nor no-thing can be responsible for existence of any kind. So what's left? Hang on to your seat, my dear atheist, because your worst nightmare is about to happen.

CHAPTER 6

CONSCIOUSNESS

GOD AND CONSCIOUSNESS

We have now come to the crucial point in our argument. We have shown that nothingness cannot be the source of infinite universes; we have shown that all things cannot be the source of infinite universes; and yet, we seem to be stuck with infinite universes. What's their source? In all eternity, there is only one other possible explanation, one other possible answer—Infinite Being, *i.e.* God.

God is the only Being that's infinite, the only Being that lasts forever; therefore, He is the only Being that can accommodate infinite universes. His Inn has infinite rooms, while all other inns will have to put up the 'No Vacancy' sign long before eternity ends, which it never does. If infinite universes are filling up eternity, and this seems to be the case, then they all must be created and sustained by an Infinite Being.

With that said and done, we can now joyfully say God exists because we have found our one true Infinity: an eternity of existence enveloped by an Infinite Being. Nothing more can possibly exist, and everything that can exist, does. Infinity's Inn is booked forever. Ooops, I guess God's Inn is going to have to put up the 'No Vacancy' sign after all: all infinite rooms are being occupied; therefore, no more rooms are left at the Inn.

You might think the story ends here, but it doesn't. Now it really gets interesting. I might have won the argument by proving the existence of an Infinite Being, but before I claim absolute victory, we need to examine this process of God and see how it operates and functions. If I show any weakness in explaining this process, I might give the atheist a way out. So without further ado, let's jump into the depths of God and see what we find.

First, before we go any further, I am going to refer to God as a He even though that's a misnomer. God is beyond He-She, Male-Female, and it's too insulting to call God an It. But until we come up with a better word to describe Him, I am going to use the masculine pronoun whenever I'm referring to God. Sorry, feminists, but I was never one to cave in to political correctness.

Settling on what to call God, we can now begin to explore the most intriguing feature of His Being. To learn what that is, all we have to do is observe ourselves. What do all humans have in common? In a word, it's Consciousness: we are all aware of our surroundings and who we are. Likewise, God has Consciousness because everything exists within

God. And since God is infinite, His Consciousness must be infinite; and since His Consciousness is infinite, Consciousness must be infinite; and since Consciousness is infinite, there must be only one Consciousness because there can be only one Being that's infinite; and since God is the only Being that's infinite, Consciousness must be God—they're one and the same! Infinite Being is Infinite Consciousness, and Infinite Consciousness is Infinite Being. God is pure, infinite Consciousness and we are all part of it.

To describe God any other way would be ludicrous because you would be giving Him a form of some kind, and there can be no form given to the Formless One. Pure Consciousness, pure Awareness, is the best way—the only way—to describe Him accurately. It is what spans eternity.

What this all means is that everything comes from Consciousness, and everything returns to Consciousness. Consciousness is the source of everything, is everything: It is Infinity Itself.

If this isn't enough to peak your interest, consider this: the Consciousness that peers through your eyes, the Consciousness that peers through my eyes is the same Consciousness as the one that creates and sustains infinite universes—we are the Consciousness that created this cosmos, can you believe it! To say otherwise is to say a boundary exists between our Consciousness and God's Consciousness, but we have already established Consciousness as our Infinite Being, so therefore there can be no boundaries within Consciousness. If we can imagine an Infinite Being, we can become an Infinite Being. It's that simple. Nothing can stop us—nothing!

I know it's hard to accept the fact that we're an Infinite Being, but it's true; the logic behind it is flawless. Consciousness is infinite and thus has been around forever. We are that Consciousness; we have no choice but to hitch a ride on that Train forever. Trying to jump off It would be like trying to run from your shadow: no matter where you go...there It is. The Consciousness peering through our eyes has been having one conscious experience after another throughout all eternity.

That's who we are. Whether we like it or not, we are here to stay—forever.

The reason we have such a hard time grasping this is because we are too caught up in our finite nature; we see ourselves as separate from each other and everything around us, and there appears to be nothing that binds us all together. Why the universe is set up this way will be explained later in the chapter, but for now we need to get beyond our finitude and separateness so that we can see into the true nature of our Being. A couple of analogies might help shed some light on the matter.

A dream is a perfect analogy to explain the Consciousness phenomenon. When we dream, what are we doing? We are dreaming about many different objects, are we not? Let's say, for example, you're dreaming about being in your living room. What do you see? You might see a couch, a couple of chairs, a table or two, a TV, lamps, candles, plants, a few paintings, a stereo system, and an old grandfather clock. All these objects seem separate and distinct from each other, and yet there is only one dreamer, one Consciousness, dreaming it all: they all emerge out of one being, and when that being wakes up, they all disappear. And so it is with Infinite Consciousness. This mighty Being dreams infinite universes, and when He's ready to wake up from a particular dream, that dream, or rather that universe, will disappear back into Himself. You could say that all of eternity is nothing but a dream, a dream that lasts forever.

Another analogy that might help us has to do with the night sky. When we look up at the sky at night, we see billions of stars scattered across the firmament. Each star has its own separate existence, and there are vast distances between one star and the next; and yet, there is only one sky sustaining them all. Eventually, all those stars will dissolve back into that one sky from which they all came. And so it is with us. We see ourselves as separate from each other, distinct from each other, and yet we all share the same Consciousness. Thus, we will eventually expand our Consciousness to a point where we will all merge together and dissolve back into that one great big sky of eternity—Infinite Consciousness.

How can we deny this? From the moment of creation, Consciousness has been in a continuous state of "unfoldment." What do you think we've been doing since the day we opened our primitive eyes—we've been expanding our Consciousness! We are constantly improving our way of life, our communication systems, and our modes of transportation; we keep finding new and wondrous ways of unlocking the secrets of nature and looking farther and farther out into the universe; we keep creating new medicines and new ways to fight disease and improve health; our architecture and engineering keeps getting better and better and more amazing as our civilization grows and expands. Soon we will be exploring our solar system, and then other parts of the galaxy, and then other galaxies, and other galaxies, and other galaxies.... When will it all end? When we are 70% conscious, 80% conscious, 90% conscious? Well hell, if we can be 90% conscious, why can't we be 95% conscious; and if we can be 95% conscious, why can't we be 100% conscious? Who or what is going to stop us? Consciousness is infinite. We are Consciousness. We can't be denied our final percentage point. Remember, no boundaries, no boundaries, no boundaries, no boundaries! That's Infinity. That's Consciousness.

To illustrate my point even further, I am going to give you a visual by using the Olympics as my setting. My reason for doing this will be self-evident shortly.

In the Olympics, records, world records, are constantly being broken. In the 100 meter dash, for example, we broke the 10 second barrier years ago, and now we're closing in on the 9 second barrier. Soon we will break that barrier, and then we will start chasing the 8 second barrier. When will we reach our maximum speed? At 7 seconds, 6 seconds, 5 seconds, 4 seconds? Well, if we can train and engineer a human body to run a 4 second 100 meter, then why can't we train it to run a 3.5 second 100 meter, a 3 second 100 meter, a 2 second 100 meter? When will it all end? I believe it will end in a scenario like this: In some distant future Olympics, our Olympians will step up to the line, and when the gun goes off...the race is over. They all crossed the finish line at the exact same time. Their time—0. They all win the gold. Our individual racers have now become one 'cosmic racer' because they all ran at the exact same speed—the speed of light. There is no difference between any of them anymore; they are one and the same, at least when it comes to running the 100 meter dash. They have

become the One Racer we've been seeking since the day the Olympics

started. And for all you time travelers out there, one of our racers

couldn't have gone faster than the speed of light, because if he did he

would have finished the race before it started and thus would have been

disqualified. (Isn't time travel bizarre.) Our racers max out at 0.

When we reach this point in our evolution, there will be no reason to

have the race anymore. Every race will end with the exact same time

every time—0. What's the point. There will be no more excitement,

no more suspense, no more drama—where's the competition! The race

will become an absolute bore. It will no longer be a viable sporting

event—it's history! Our 100 meter dash will finally come to an end

and cease to exist once and for all. The end.

And so it is with the Consciousness Game. Our Game is never over

until it's over. And when is it over? It's over when our Consciousness

reaches an infinite state of being. Since there is no being greater than

an Infinite Being, we can go no further than God. As our racers max

out at 0, we max out at Infinity. When we reach this stage of development, all our individual I's will coalesce into one Cosmic I, the Creator and Master of all. At that point, we will be able to take the universe by its reins and ride it into Infinity; and as we pass through the pearly-gates on our blazing saddles, the universe will burst into a blaze of infinite glory, melting into that fiery Sea of Consciousness—Us. The end.

This is how the process of God works. It begins when a universe emerges out of His Being and starts to expand and grow. Eventually it becomes aware of itself, and this awareness grows and grows until it becomes what it always was—Infinite Consciousness. Once Consciousness becomes infinite, there's no need for the universe anymore; it has served its purpose; it too will become what it always was—Infinite Being. Our mighty Being has awakened, and the objects in His dream—the universe—have disappeared back into Himself. The process is over....

Until it starts again. It's an endless process that repeats itself throughout eternity: infinite universes bubbling out of this boiling Sea of Consciousness, only to recede back into It at their appointed times. It's never-ending, without beginning or end, forever and ever.

To me, this is what's so mind-boggling about this process: it's always been going on and we never catch on to it. God, Consciousness, has created infinite universes, journeyed through infinite universes, evolved infinite universes back into Himself, and yet look at us: we act like this is the first universe we've ever experienced. This is what I find so amazing; it always seems like the first time every time Consciousness creates and experiences a new universe, even though infinite universes have already come and gone. How bizarre is that? Only God can come up with a plan as glorious and magnificent as this one. It's sheer brilliance, pure genius, a total masterpiece; in a word, it's perfect. It can never get any better than this. We will forever find ourselves lost in a universe, never being able to find our way out until we wake up. And how do we wake up? By becoming Infinite.

Our spiritual masters of the past understood quite well this whole cosmic phenomenon. The *rishis* of ancient India saw the universe as Maya, a cosmic illusion, which meant there was no permanence whatsoever to the universe. The Being behind the illusion is what was permanent and everlasting, and they called this Being Brahman. As we grow spiritually, the *rishis* taught us we would eventually see through this illusion and into our true nature. Once we become our true Self, the universe would pop like a bubble and we would become Brahman, that is, God, pure Consciousness, Infinite Being. It doesn't matter which term we use because they all have the exact same meaning: they mean 'That which there is no beyond'. Once we become That, the illusion is over. Five thousand years ago and some of us already understood this, which just goes to show that Consciousness can reveal its mystical secrets to anyone at any point in time, even to me...hopefully.

WHY?

Now that we have a clear picture how the process of God works, we can now ask the question everyone wants to ask—why? Why does God do it? Why does He create infinite universes? Why does He continually lose Himself in universe after universe after universe after universe, only to find Himself again and again and again and again? There is only one reason why He does it—to complete His Infinity.

For God to be truly infinite, He must not only experience Himself, but also every possible universe, every possible being, every possible experience, every possible pathway to enlightenment. This is the only way He can complete the infinity of His Consciousness. Anything less would limit His Infinity, and that is not allowed because there can be no limits to Infinity. Therefore, God must spend forever creating everything possible and experiencing everything possible. Such is the way of Infinity.

Even if He wanted to, God couldn't have it any other way. Any other way would bring a beginning to the process, and there can be no beginning to Infinity. Not even God, in all His infinite wisdom, can create a beginning, that is, a first universe. Like the 'thing theory' and 'nothing theory', He would have to exist forever first, and since it takes forever for forever to come to an end, He could never get to a first universe. So what does He do? He does both: He exists forever as Himself, and at the same time He creates and experiences infinite universes. His Infinity is covered.

There is, however, an interesting side note to all this. It is possible to actually experience a point before a first universe, but we won't get there by going back into an infinite past; we will get there through a state of Consciousness. When we evolve into Infinite Being, we will experience the ultimate state of Consciousness. There will be no universes in that state, no anything, only the pure White Light of Consciousness—our Divine Self. So, in a way, there is a point before a first universe, consciously speaking, that is.

Of course, Consciousness will be caught dreaming once again, lost in another universe, wondering what it all means and what is it all for, is there a purpose to existence or isn't there, does God exist or doesn't He, is there an ultimate destiny or just a meaningless end to a meaningless existence, and so on, and so on, and so on. Sound familiar?

HOW?

Now that we've explained why God does it, we can now try to figure out how He does it—how is He able to become infinite beings experiencing infinite experiences within infinite universes. There is only one way He can do it: by becoming finite and losing Himself in a finite state of Consciousness. Let me explain.

Let's say, for example, God wants to climb Mt. Everest. Granted, Everest emerged out of His Being; granted, it will dissolve back into His Being; granted, His Being permeates every pore of the rock; but how is God going to know what it is like to climb Everest from bottom to top unless He turns Himself into a finite form and becomes a mountain climber. Only then can He experience the climb, only then can He experience the danger, only then can He experience the exhilaration of making it to the top of the highest mountain in the world. But even this isn't enough. God has to do more. He has to make the experience real, believable. The only way He can do this is to leave His Infiniteness and lose Himself in a finite state of Consciousness. By becoming a being with limited awareness, God no longer sees Himself as God but as a mountain climber climbing a mountain fraught with danger. This is what gives the experience its realness, its seal of authenticity. Now it is a full—fledged experience, ready to be filed away in the archives of Infinity as an actual experience after the experience has ended.

If, on the other hand, God didn't lose Himself in a finite state of Consciousness, then the experience couldn't become real, because God would be pretending He was a mountain climber, not a finite being actually believing he was a mountain climber. Thus the experience wouldn't be authentic; it would be a fake, a farce, and wouldn't be included in the realm of infinite experiences. In order to authenticate the experience, and thus make it one of the infinite experiences out there, God must lose Himself in a finite being and forget who He is. Then the adventure begins and the experience becomes real.

In short, all that is really going on here is a cosmic theatrical production. God creates a universe and then turns it into a stage. He then turns Himself into myriad actors performing on that stage. Each actor has his or her own set of experiences, and each actor has his or her own pathway to enlightenment. When we expand this to include infinite universes, we have the following: infinite actors, infinite experiences, and infinite pathways to enlightenment. In other words, it is all God. It is His Infinity. It is His way of playing hide-and-seek with Himself forever and ever.

This in a nutshell is how the Game of God is played, commonly known as the Consciousness Game. In His own ingenious way, God creates us then becomes us, and through us He is able to explore the infinite domain of His Consciousness. And through this exploration, the Consciousness that we are will eventually find Its way back Home to Its original state—God.

When you think about it, is there any other way God can play the Game? Is there any other way He can spend eternity? Is there any other way He can exist without becoming eternally bored or insane?

Think about it for a moment. Experiencing His own Glorious Light I'm sure is a wonderful experience for God, but what does He do after that? If He didn't do anything else, He probably would end up sounding like a frustrated little kid, crying, "Mommy, I'm bored. I want to play and there is nothing to do." The only solution: "Go play in your universe, sweetheart. That should occupy your time for the next 20 billion years or so." Multiply this by infinite universes and God's problem is solved for good.

STATES OF CONSCIOUSNESS AND BEYOND THE HUMAN FORM

There is one other aspect of God's Infinity we need to address, and that has to do with His different levels of Consciousness. Besides creating and experiencing everything possible, God has to experience every state of Consciousness possible. This applies not only to human states, but to all other states as well, even animal states. That's right, people, the Consciousness peering through a deer's eyes, the Consciousness peering through a bear's eyes, the Consciousness peering through your pet's eyes is the same Consciousness as the one that creates and sustains infinite universes. From your cat's meow to a lion's roar, from an amoeba to God Himself, it is all one Being, one Consciousness, experiencing and exploring existence in an infinite variety of ways. To say otherwise would mean there is a boundary line between God-Consciousness and all other states of Consciousness, but we already know there can be no boundaries within an Infinite Consciousness. Therefore, God can become it all, experience it all. If He can imagine a deer, He can become a deer. It's that simple. To deny Him this right is to deny Him His own Infinity.

This is not to say that a deer can become infinitely aware. All it means is that the Consciousness peering through the deer's eyes will become infinitely aware. For that to happen, Consciousness will have to seek out other forms, forms like us. The reason why we are so special is because we are in a state of Consciousness that can imagine an Infinite Being. Imagining an Infinite Being is the first step in becoming an Infinite Being, and we are well on our way. Our own primitive mythology (check out Joseph Campbell's 'Primitive Mythology') suggests our Consciousness became aware of God around 250–400 thousand years ago, so we have been at it a long time already. It might take millions, if not billions, of more years to complete the process, to turn this universe back into God, but it will happen, Infinity decrees it. Will humans be around at that point? Probably not. But Consciousness will be, and that's who we are.

We shouldn't be shocked at the idea of humans not being around in the future. Remember, we are not the forms we inhabit; we are the Consciousness that inhabits the forms. Throughout earth's history Consciousness has used many different forms to advance Itself. The first signs of awareness began with bacteria, then fish, then reptiles, then dinosaurs, then mammals, then apes, now us. We are the latest craze in the evolution of Consciousness, but I seriously doubt we will be the craze of the future. But so what. Whatever new form Consciousness takes, that's who we will be. The Consciousness peering through the new being's eyes will be the same Consciousness as the one that peers through our eyes, that peered through the dinosaur's eyes, that swam the primordial waters. It is all one continuum of Consciousness, and we are all of it, from the first state to the infinite state.

So there's no need to worry, no need to fret, if tomorrow we are no longer here. Think of the human form as being nothing more than the skin of a snake. When the snake sheds his skin for a new one, he is still the same snake; nothing changes except for his new apparel. And so it is with Consciousness. If Consciousness sheds the human skin for a new one, It will still be the same Consciousness, the same Awareness. That's us. We are the eyes of the snake, not his skin.

Hearing that we might not be the only players at the table has probably bruised a lot of human egos. I can already hear some of you screaming, "How can you say that about us? You said we were the first beings to become aware of God, you said our Consciousness can evolve into God, you said there is no being greater than God, so how can there be any beings greater than us? Are we not the top of the food chain, or rather, the top of the Consciousness chain?"

Human arrogance at its best. First, I was referring only to this planet when I said we were the first beings to become aware of God; and second, just because we have become aware of God doesn't mean we are the only beings in the universe to have done so. There are galaxies that are millions and millions of years older than ours, so it's quite possible that there are beings out there who are much more consciously advanced and have a greater awareness of God than we do. But even if that's the case, the Consciousness peering through their eyes is the same Consciousness as the one peering through our eyes. They too are staring out at the universe and wondering what it all means and what is it all for. They too have evolved from lower forms and will continue to evolve into newer forms as time goes on. This process will continue until Consciousness develops forms that can integrate the universe, that is, create a network that ties all self-aware, conscious beings in the universe together. This will allow the tentacles of Consciousness to stretch across the universe, strengthening it, unifying it, turning it into a cosmic brain, so to speak. And when Consciousness finally devises forms that can make every cosmic neuron in the universe fire at once, this universe will have reached its maximum potential. Consciousness

will become infinite once again, and the universe will shine like a

bright, celestial star, radiating the pure White Light of Consciousness.

And don't be dismayed if this magical moment is still millions or

billions of years away yet. Getting there is half the fun. Remember, for

God to complete His Infinity, He must experience all that there is to

experience. So what's the hurry, what's the rush? Let Consciousness

explore this universe thoroughly. It will find its way back home

eventually. It always does. But for now, enjoy the adventure.

REINCARNATION

I would like to take a brief moment and talk about the theory of

reincarnation. Now I am not here to advocate Buddhist reincarnation,

Hindu reincarnation, or any other type of religious reincarnation. The

reason why I want to leave religion out of it is because religions are

fighting amongst themselves enough as it is already, and I don't want to create another firestorm by taking one side over another when it comes to reincarnation. Therefore, I have come up with my own version of reincarnation based on the laws of Infinity and the relationship between Consciousness and form. My reasoning is as follows:

In all eternity, there is only one Being that is infinite, and that Being is God. Every other type of existence is finite and has a form to it of some kind. We, for example, have the human form. So the question naturally arises as to what happens to the Consciousness peering through our eyes after our bodies die. It has to go somewhere because Consciousness has been around forever. So where does it go? If Consciousness isn't ready to become infinite yet, if the universe isn't ready to come to an end yet, and we already know that nothingness doesn't exist out there in Infinity Land, then the only option left for Consciousness is to seek out another form. It has no choice but to jump from form to form, and continue to jump from form to form, until It finally jumps into the Formless State. It is there where the jumping stops. If what I've just described is reincarnation, then so be it. If not, Consciousness is still going to jump.

EXPERIENCING THE WHITE LIGHT

Throughout human history, there have been stories of people actually experiencing a oneness with God or being bathed in an ocean of White Light. The *rishis* of ancient India, Christian saints, mystics, and other spiritual people have all made such claims. I have no reason to doubt these stories, and why should I? Each and every one of us has the innate capability of busting through all the imaginary boundaries of Consciousness and into the Boundless State. We know this to be true because Consciousness is infinite and has no boundaries; everything exists within It, even the infinite state. The fact that there are people who experience this state proves my point. What I find interesting about all this, though, is not that these people experience the White Light, but that they come back from the experience. Why is that? Why, after experiencing the greatest experience known to man, do they even bother to come back? Why don't they leave their bodies for good? Why don't they stay out there permanently? The answer is simple: they can't.

Experiencing the White Light is one thing, turning the whole universe into the White Light is quite another. It is going to take a lot more time and energy to pull that off. The people who experience the White Light are merely precursors of what is to come; they have experienced some distant, eschatological event, but they will never be able to sustain that event on a permanent basis until we all experience it together. When every spiritual being in the universe experience the White Light simultaneously, we will all enter the same state of Consciousness. There will be no you, I, or we in that state, only one Universal Consciousness; the many will have become the One. In that moment, the universe will be consumed by the White Light the way a log is consumed by fire. All that will remain will be the blinding White Light, and it will be at that time that the Consciousness peering through our eyes will be able to sustain the White Light permanently, not a moment before.

And after this great, climatic end to the universe, need I remind you what happens next—that's right, folks, we get to do it all over again, and again, and again, forevermore. Ain't it grand.

HEAVEN

There are probably some of you out there who don't like this idea of going from one universe to another forever and ever. You want to find a place where everything is good and nice, where the lion lies down with the lamb and everyone is lovey-dovey with each other. This sounds like a wonderful place, and it might even exist somewhere within Consciousness, but to spend forever there—come on! Don't you think there will come a time when you will want to here the lion roar once again, to see him behave like a wildcat instead of a pussycat. Where would all the thrill and excitement go if we knew every situation was always going to end with a 'Happy Face'? Wouldn't heaven become monotonous after a while? As the old saying goes, too much of

a good thing is...too much!

No, I don't think heaven is meant to be like this at all. God is an

adventurer. He wants to experience existence in as many ways as

possible. He wants to experience the thrill of not knowing how it is all

going to turn out until the end, and when it ends, He's ready for another

adventure. It's like us and movies. Would we enjoy a movie if we

already knew how it ended? Would we stop going to movies because

we already saw one? Of course not. We keep going to movies because

we enjoy the adventure each movie offers and not knowing how each

movie is going to turn out until the end. To put and end to this, to put

an end to the adventure, would not be heaven but a living hell. No

thank you.

So what is heaven then? I believe heaven is simply this: to have an

infinite amount of time to experience an infinite amount of experiences.

What more could a God possibly want.

WHAT IS TO BECOME OF FAITH

What is faith? According to Webster, faith is a 'firm belief in something for which there is no proof', but if I have proven beyond the shadow of a doubt that God exists, does that not then take the wind out of faith, and if I have taken the wind out of faith, does it not then stand to reason that the role faith plays in our lives will be greatly diminished, almost to the point of irrelevancy? Not at all. Faith will always be crucial to our spiritual development. All I am trying to do is redirect faith, not do away with it. Instead of having faith that God exists, which we now know to be true, we should have faith that we can become Him, that we can evolve into His State of Consciousness. It's like a mountain and a mountain climber. Just because someone has discovered Everest doesn't make the climb any easier. The mountain climber still needs to have faith that he can overcome all obstacles and make it to the top of the world. The spiritual path is no different. Knowing that God exists doesn't make the journey any easier. It is still filled with many fears, doubts and uncertainties, and since we are in a finite state of Consciousness, we will never know for sure what lies ahead. That's where faith comes in. We need to have faith that God will show us the way, that He will guide us across the pernicious waters all the way to the eternal shores of being, where the glorious White Light awaits our presence. Without it we would be forever lost at sea. So there is no need to panic, my friends, faith is still alive and well out there in Infinity Land.

QUANTUM PHYSICS AND CONSCIOUSNESS

Before we end the chapter, I would like to take a few moments and talk about a strange and bizarre new science known as quantum physics. The reason I want to spend some time talking about it is because in its own strange way it describes quite well the nature of God. Whether or not quantum physicists had God in mind when they started this new science is not what's important here; what they discovered is. I would like to touch on three points quantum physics makes. They are: Consciousness, the wave-particle duality, and how the electron moves between orbits. Let's start with Consciousness first.

Quantum physicists were the first scientists to include Consciousness in any scientific experiment. They realized that you could never completely separate the observer from the observed, the subject from the object, the experimenter from the experiment. Rather, there was interconnectedness between the person performing the experiment and the objects of the experiment. I've always had a hard time trying to understand what this meant, but after hearing about a particular experiment, it all became very clear to me.

The experiment I'm referring to had to do with a female professor and her students. The object of the experiment was to see if her students could tell when they were being observed by her when she wasn't in the room. To run the experiment, the professor did the following: she put a closed circuit video camera in the room where her students were and hooked it up to a TV monitor in her own private room. This way she could observe the students whenever she wanted to by turning the monitor on. Her students, on the other hand, could never tell if the camera was on or off.

After running the experiment over a several week period, she found that her students became very adept at knowing when they were being observed. She was so excited about the results that she told a male colleague about it. Being somewhat curious, he decided to run the same experiment, and his results...sucked! On hearing about his debacle, the female professor just threw up her arms and said, "I guess it all has to do with the person running the experiment."

Not knowing the two professors personally, I can't say what actually happened, but I bet you I can come up with a scenario that is pretty accurate. When it came to the female professor, she probably was more involved in the experiment than her male colleague was. She most likely paid very close attention to the students whenever she turned the monitor on, watching their every move, studying their behavior, trying to determine when or if they knew they were being observed. She might've even tried to communicate telepathically with them. Whatever the case, it is probably a safe bet to assume that her

Consciousness was deeply involved in the experiment. She saw herself as a participator in the event, having a connection with her students in the deepest layers of Consciousness. This, I'm sure, was crucial in helping the students sense her presence whenever the camera was turned on.

Her male colleague, on the other hand, probably had a different approach. Whenever he turned the monitor on, he might've poured himself a cup of coffee, ate a donut, or was thinking about a very important paper he was working on. He might've been looking at the TV screen during all this, but his mind, or rather his Consciousness, was elsewhere. He probably didn't think much about his non-involvement because he didn't see himself as an integral part of the experiment. He saw himself simply as an objective observer, having no connection whatsoever to the students, only a disconnect. His job was to record the times when the monitor was on and compare those times to the times when the students thought they were being observed, that's all. This non-participation by the male professor is what made it extremely difficult, if not impossible, for the students to sense his presence.

From this one example, we can see what quantum physicists are talking about when they say Consciousness is part of the experiment. It can never be fully detached from the tests being conducted because It influences the tests; It will always be a determining factor in any eventual outcome.

I believe quantum physicists are right on target here, but if I might be so bold, I don't think they go far enough. I believe they will find out someday that Consciousness isn't part of the experiment—It is the experiment! By penetrating the depths of Consciousness, we will be able to penetrate the depths of matter and unleash the full force of the universe, transforming it into the Infinite. When that time arrives, Consciousness and the universe, Experimenter and experiment, will merge together and become one undifferentiated whole. The experiment will be over at that point, and it will be time to close up shop. Next experiment, please.

Another interesting aspect of quantum physics is the wave-particle duality of matter. This is a theory that says matter can be both a particle and a wave at the same time. By observing an electron, for example, quantum physicists found out that there was a dual nature to its existence. In one state, it functioned as a wave that spread out across the space-time continuum, having no exact location anywhere. In another state, it functioned as a microscopic particle that had an exact location within the space-time continuum. These two complementary aspects of the electron is what made the quantum physicists come up with the wave-particle duality of matter.

Even if I wanted to, I couldn't describe God any better than this. The wave-particle duality of matter illustrates perfectly the dual nature of God. In one state, He is a wave of pure, infinite Consciousness, pure, infinite Energy, spanning eternity, existing everywhere at once. In another state, He is a Being of infinite particles, infinite universes, each universe existing at a particular point within the wave the way a water molecule exists at a particular point within a vast ocean. As a wave, God experiences the ocean, His uncreated, infinite Self. As a particle, He experiences a water molecule, His created, finite self. This dual nature of God, His infinite side and His finite side, is what completes the totality of His Being, just as the wavelike and particle-like aspects of an electron completes the totality of its being.

It should also be noted that God's duality can be expressed within our own universe as well. In one state, God is a wave of Consciousness that spreads out across the whole space-time continuum, having no exact location anywhere, existing at all points simultaneously. In another state, He is countless particles of Consciousness, particles like you and me, each particle having an exact location in space and in time. As a wave, God experiences the whole space-time continuum at once. As a particle, He experiences a particular point within the space-time continuum. I will go into this in more detail in the next chapter when I run you through a thought experiment, but for now just accept the fact that God exists at every point in space and time—NOW!

Another interesting point about the wave-particle duality is this idea about electrons existing as probability waves. What this means is that until an electron is observed by Consciousness (an observer), it exists as a probability wave, spreading out over a large area of space, existing at all probable locations simultaneously. Once an observation is made, the wave collapses and an electron appears at a particular point in space; all possibilities have collapsed into one actuality. In other words, reality has been found.

From this one tiny example, we can see how probability waves function when it comes to Consciousness and infinite universes. All universes are mere probability waves, infinite possibilities within Consciousness. When Consciousness zeroes in on a particular wave, the wave collapses and a particle appears, *i.e.* a universe. Now we have an actual existence that Consciousness can experience and explore, much in the same way a scientist experiences and explores a molecule when looking at it through a microscope. Our universe is one such molecule. It is a wave that has collapsed into reality, and now it's being observed under the microscope of Consciousness. This observation-participation will continue until the universe disappears back into the Infinite; and when that happens, another probability wave, another universe, will collapse into reality, continuing the journey, continuing the adventure, through Consciousness.

The last point I want to bring up about quantum physics has to do with how an electron changes orbits. I should warn you, though, that what I'm about to say is going to sound so strange and bizarre that you might consider me certifiable, if you haven't already done so. The reason why I say this is because after learning how an electron moves between orbits, I have come up with a theory about reality that is beyond belief. Is my theory correct? My intuition says yes, but all I can do is present my argument to you and let you decide.

First, before I explain what my theory is, I should first explain what a quantum leap is. A quantum leap is the way an electron changes orbits inside an atom. An electron has many orbits, and when it's orbiting around the nucleus of an atom in one orbit, it can all of a sudden without warning jump ship and leap to another orbit. Thus the term 'quantum leap.' This leap is instantaneous, and what's peculiar about all this is that we don't know how or where the electron leaps. In one instant it is here, then there, but we don't have a clue how it got from here to there. Physicists say it jumps, but what does that mean? All they can tell us is that when an electron jumps it doesn't move between orbits, meaning, it doesn't travel across the space-time continuum. If an electron doesn't jump across space and time to get to its destination, then how does it get from orbit to orbit? Where is that electron in that instantaneous moment between here and there? This is a baffling mystery with no satisfactory answer, which forces me to come up with a theory of my own. Could it be that the electron bypasses the whole space-time continuum altogether? Could it be that the electron moves through Consciousness instead?

Before you dismiss this out of hand, consider the following: sub-atomic particles are the first elements of existence that emerge out of the Infinite, which means they are closer to the Infinite than any other form of existence; they are the point where the Infinite ends and the finite begins. If they were any smaller, they would vanish from existence altogether and return to the infinite state of being—Consciousness. They have no other place to go.

A good analogy here would be to compare sub-atomic particles to the tiniest bubbles of foam floating on the surface of the sea. These tiny bubbles are the smallest particles of existence that can remain afloat without going under. Any smaller and they would drop beneath the surface and disappear out of sight, just as sub-atomic particles would disappear back into the Sea of the Infinite. You can't get any smaller than these guys and still retain an individual identity. At some point the point will become too small and it will simply vanish from existence, dissolving into the sea if it's a bubble of foam, or dissolving into Infinite Being if it's a sub-atomic particle.

Another known fact about sub-atomic particles is that they all break down into energy vibrations that blink in and out of existence countless times per second. Our senses are way too slow to notice this given the incredible rate of speed at which this is all happening. What are senses do pick up is a stable reality, when in reality all of reality is blinking in and out of existence continuously. The whole cosmos, it appears, is nothing more than one big flashing light. To quote Deepak Chopra: 'But you could never capture that electron anyway, since it too breaks down into energy vibrations that wink in and out of existence millions of times per second. Therefore the whole universe is a quantum mirage, winking in and out of existence millions of times per second'. (From his book, 'How to know God.')

This behavior at the quantum level might well explain how an electron can jump orbits. In the 'blinking in' stage, an electron is an electron, representing the stable reality we all see and experience through our senses. In the 'blinking out' stage, an electron disappears from reality altogether. Where does it go? Being so close to the surface of the Infinite, could it be that it vibrantly dips beneath the surface and enters the infinite state of being (pure Consciousness). Once there, it could relocate anywhere instantaneously because the Infinite is everywhere at once. Thus, an electron could change orbits without traveling across the space-time continuum. All it would have to do is dip, and this dipping would happen so fast that an electron could disappear and reappear before we would even notice it missing. All we would notice is that it has changed orbits.

Now some of you might think what's the big deal here since we're only dealing with infinitesimal distances. It's true that the distances we are talking about are infinitesimally small, but you have to remember that everything is relative. On its own scale, the distance between an electron and the nucleus of an atom is farther than the distance between the earth and the sun. Granted, electronic orbits are closer to each other than they are to the nucleus, but huge jumps are still being made. An average jump between orbits is probably equivalent to jumping from here to the moon—instantaneously! Not bad for one leap.

If this is how the microworld jumps, then can we find any evidence of this kind of jumping in the macroworld? The paranormal and paranormal abilities might shed some light on this matter.

One example of paranormal ability is telekinesis. This is the ability to move objects without touching them. How someone does this is with his or her Consciousness. By some type of conscious ability or development, the person is able to merge with a particular object, become one with it so to speak, and move it to wherever he or she wants it to go. This is undoubtedly an impressive ability, but even telekinesis has its own stages of development.

If someone puts a stone on a table and makes it move slowly across the table, we would say this person has psychic abilities but that they were in the early stages of development. If another person puts a stone on the table and makes it move faster across the table, we would say this person is more advanced. If someone else puts on a stone on the table and makes it move swiftly across the table, we would say this person is very advanced. What would make a person the most advanced, the master? I believe he would have to be able to do something like this: he would put a stone on the table, and as everyone who was watching blinked an eye, the stone would already be at the other end of the table. Everybody would be standing there flabbergasted, wondering what just happened. They would turn to each other and say, "How did that happen? I didn't see it move. Did you see it move? I didn't see it move." The reason why they didn't see it move is because the stone didn't move across the space-time continuum; it moved through Consciousness instead; and since Consciousness is infinite and everywhere at once, the stone can be anywhere at once. In this instance, the stone was placed at the other end of the table, but it could have just as easily been placed on the moon, on Mars, or on some other planet in the farthest regions of the universe.

If you think what I just said is impossible, then let me try to broaden your horizon. At the beginning of the book I mentioned I have been practicing *yoga* off and on over the years, and the ability I just described is commonplace within the *yoga* world. The stories are endless. Here are a few examples.

In one instance, a student and his master were living in a cave in Tibet. One day, after a couple of months of living there, a thought flashed in the student's mind: he wished he had brought his diary with him so that he could note down a few experiences. His master sensed this and said, "Do you want me to get it for you?" The student casually replied, "Yes, and a few pencils, too." Suddenly, his diary and three pencils were before him.

In another instance, a sewing machine salesman doubted such abilities existed. He went to visit a master *yogi* and told him that if he could make a sewing machine appear from his store this instant, he would become a believer and follow him anywhere. The *yogi* granted him his wish. The startled salesman looked at the sewing machine and he could tell it came from his store. He became a believer. He picked up the sewing machine and headed back to the store, but before he could get there he was stopped by the police. Apparently, the store owner had already reported it stolen. O the fate that befalls the doubting Thomas'.

Besides moving inanimate objects, it seems *yogis* can also move people this way. There's a story about a group of children who wanted to attend a religious festival, but they had no way of getting there. The local *yogi* approached the children and told them they should touch him, and when they did, the whole group was instantly transported to the festival, 150 miles away. Another *yogi* was known to move from place to place in the Himalayas with his disciples. Whenever it was time to move, the *yogi* would lift his bamboo staff into the air, say a few words, and the whole group would vanish, immediately appearing at the next location.

If these stories are not enough to knock your socks off, *yogis* can take it one step further: it seems they can make objects appear out of nowhere. At a religious banquet, a student wanted to test his master's abilities. He knew tangerines were out of season, so he asked his master if he could make a few tangerines appear on the table. The master told him to look at the fruit bowl, and lo and behold the bowl was filled with tangy tangerines. The student grabbed one, peeled it, bit into it and was amazed at how tasty it was.

In another strange event, a young *yogi* was led into the icy Himalaya night by a distant voice. For hours he walked through the forest, and as he came to a turn in the path, the night was suddenly lit up by a bright light in the distance. As he approached the light, he came upon a shimmering, golden palace. He was awe-struck by the beauty and splendor of this mystical place. He entered its domain and wandered about the palace rooms. He came across countless jewels and gems, landscaped gardens, tranquil pools, towering archways, exquisite works of art. He marveled at everything, touched everything, and they all passed the sensory experience test.

He continued onward and entered an immense hall. There, sitting in a lotus posture on a golden thrown, was his master. The *yogi* knelt on the shining floor at his master's feet.

His guru smiled and said, "I was the distant voice you heard. I wanted to bring you here because you once expressed the desire to enjoy the beauties of a palace. I am now satisfying your wish."

After saying these words, the master performed a few rituals, and then he let the young *yogi* spend the rest of the night exploring the many splendors of this enchanting mansion. In the morning the two met again, and the master told his young disciple to close his eyes. When he reopened them, the palace and master were gone.

All these events I have just described took place in India, and they are well documented in two books: 'Living With The Himalayan Masters' and 'The Autobiography Of A Yogi'. You can choose to believe these stories or not. But if you choose not to believe, then you have to ask yourself two questions. First, why would *yogis* lie? They all live very austere lives, and the last thing they seek is fame and fortune. For the most part, they just want to be left alone. Making up stories and telling lies would serve them no purpose whatsoever. And second, to choose not to believe is to put limits on Consciousness, and since God is pure Consciousness, are you not ultimately putting limits on God? Do you really want to go there? Think about it.

For those who do believe, you're probably wondering how in the hell do they do it? Great question. *Yogis* tell us it all has to do with the willful powers of Consciousness. They say if you will something within Consciousness, it will manifest itself in the physical world. What this means is that through the power of Consciousness, and through the power of Consciousness alone, we can make anything happen. If we will a stone to the other end of the table, it will instantly appear there. If we will a golden palace into existence, it will instantly appear before our very eyes. If we will ourselves to another location, we're already there. This ability will take time to develop, but our destiny awaits us.

The reason why all this is possible is because of the nature of Consciousness. Consciousness is the source of everything, creates everything, flows through everything, is everything, makes every atom and sub-atomic particle vibrate with energy. Your field of vision are not objects that are separate from you—they are you. If you want a distant tree branch to sway back and forth, it will, because your Consciousness flows through the bark, through the leaves, through the sap, through the elemental particles themselves. You don't need to move across the space-time continuum to move that branch—you're already there! Will it and it will move.

Maybe this is what Jesus meant when he said we could move mountains. A mountain is not separate from our Consciousness; it is part of our Consciousness. Our Consciousness flows through every atom of every mountain. If we want to move a particular mountain, then in that instantaneous moment when its atoms are blinking out of existence and into the Infinite, our Consciousness can will those atoms back into existence at another location, all before our senses register anything. Let Thy Will be done.

In short, it appears all objects of Consciousness are continuously blinking in and out of existence and in and out of the Infinite, that Substance peering through your eyes. While objects are in that Substance, you can will them anywhere, reconstitute them into any shape you so desire. You've heard about people having the ability to bend spoons by touching them. A true master would only have to will a spoon to bend and its atoms would change directions immediately. If you want objects to appear out of nowhere, the willful powers of your Consciousness will make atoms instantly shape themselves into any shape your will desires. If you want to visit a far away place, your conscious will make the atoms of your body instantly appear at the destination of your choice. It's a mastery that only Consciousness can achieve.

You should take a crack at this ability the next time you're out walking. When you come upon a stone, blink and see if it moves. It won't, but give it time. It might not happen in this lifetime, but as your Consciousness jumps from form to form, this ability will slowly grow and develop, and there will come a time when moving and manipulating objects will be as easy as moving and manipulating your baby finger. This ability will continue to grow until you, I and everyone else become one unified, universal Consciousness. When that time arrives, we will blink this universe out of existence in an instant, and we will blink another universe into existence an instant later. Happy blinking.

Before I make my last point about quantum jumping, it just occurred to me that I'm going to have to make a slight change to my story about the Olympic racers and the 100 meter dash. In the future, there might be a brilliant scientist who has created a device that can measure the time it takes for our racers to streak down the track at the speed of light. His device might be able to come up with readings that show our first place runner ran the 100 meter dash in .0000001, just edging out the second place guy by .000000000000000123. With such precise measurement of time, the only way our racers could ever run an absolute 0 100 meter dash would be by willing themselves to the finish line via Consciousness. As the gun was going off, the atoms of their bodies would already be rematerializing at the other end of the track.

Our scientist would be at a loss for words to explain what just happened because his highly advanced machine didn't record anything: no speed, no time—nothing! The screen was completely blank. "How did they do that?" he would undoubtedly mumble to himself. There was no evidence of them moving down the track, no evidence of them moving across the space-time continuum. How did they get from point A to point B? They got there by bypassing the space-time continuum altogether and traveling by the instantaneous transport of Consciousness. Moving by such means allowed our racers to move undetected across the radar of time. All our scientist could do after witnessing an event like this is throw up his arms and say, "The racers ran the race in no time at all." Our absolute 0 is back in play.

The last point I want to make about electronic jumping has to do with this notion of electrons changing orbits randomly. According to physicists, an electron can change orbits without warning and for no good reason; it's all based on the purely random activity of the quantum world. Where or when an electron jumps is anyone's guess. I beg to differ with this notion. To me, saying something is random is the same as saying we don't know what's going on. I believe there is a reason why electrons behave the way they do, and I would like to share this reasoning with you.

To understand my point, try to imagine the universe as one big body, and all the atoms in the universe are the cells of that body. When atoms are agitated, the electrons are in higher energy states; when atoms are quiet, the electrons are in lower energy states.

Now, let's say we've created a new technology that can map out the whole universe and determine its state on any given day. For example, on one particular day we find that the universe is in a very agitated state: there are more ferocious solar flares than normal, more supernovae than normal, more comets crashing into planets than normal, more earthquakes and volcanic eruptions than normal and so on and so on. The next day the complete opposite is true: there are fewer solar flares, fewer supernovae, fewer cosmic crashes, *etc. etc.*

When we analyze all the data with our new technology, we find that on the first day all the electrons in the universe were for the most part in higher energy states, and on the second day they were in lower energy states. In other words, the electrons reflected the state of the universe at a particular moment in time. There was nothing haphazard about their jumping whatsoever; their behavior was dictated by events in the universe, not randomness.

Now, let's apply this thinking to our day to day existences. Haven't we all experienced moments of chaos and calm in our own lives. I know I have. When I'm driving my taxi, there are days when my customers are very nice and polite—and great tippers! The traffic flows smoothly, nobody is trying to cut anyone off, few accidents are happening, people are courteous and considerate, police aren't giving out many tickets, and all seems right with the world. Other days, though, are a living nightmare. Customers are rude and nasty—and lousy tippers! People are cutting each other off, accidents are happening everywhere, sirens can be heard all over the city, police are pulling people over left and right, traffic is a mess, cars are breaking down, animals are lying dead in the street, and on and on the nightmare goes. If we expand this to include the whole city, we will probably find that emergency rooms are busier than normal, bosses are jumping all over their employees, customer service reps at all the major stores are hearing one complaint after another from mean-spirited, angry customers, kids are driving moms nuts, and husbands and wives are at each other's throats. In other words, it's just another wonderful day in the neighborhood.

What's going on here is that our actions and behaviors are expressing the mood of the universe at a particular moment. On some days the universe cops an attitude and the atoms become agitated, causing electrons to jump to higher orbits and making us all feel moody, irritable, mean and nasty. On other days the universe settles down and the atoms become quiet, allowing electrons to jump to lower orbits and making us all feel calm, peaceful, considerate and kind.

Of course, most days aren't this chaotic or calm. It is probably the case that most days are a balancing act between both extremes. If we scan the universe on any given day with our new technological equipment, we will probably find that there are as many electronic jumps to higher energy states as there are to lower energy states. In other words, there's a stable, rhythmic beat to the universe, just as there is a stable, rhythmic beat to the human heart. On some days the heart rate is up, on other days it's down, but for the most part the heart is stable and beating rhythmically. And so is the universe. This equilibrium is what keeps the universe in check and allows Consciousness to evolve Itself. Without this stability, Consciousness may never be able to find its way back home.

The point I'm trying to make about all this is that all the atoms and sub-atomic particles in the universe are reacting to the behavior of their body, and their body is the universe. When atoms become agitated or quiet, when electrons jump north or south, they are responding to the whole activity of the universe at that exact moment, and distance is never a factor. Look at our own bodies, for example. When we stub a toe, we are talking about a very small area of the body, and yet the whole body reacts and moves when our toe makes contact with a table leg. If we scan the whole body at that exact moment, we will probably find that most atoms became agitated and most electrons jumped to higher orbits. Likewise, when a supernova happens, it happens in a very small area of the universe, and yet the whole universe reacts to it by shaking up all the atoms and electrons. Granted, the atoms and electrons that are farther away from the supernova will be less affected by it, but the effects will still be felt to a certain degree. And the more supernovae there are, the bigger the effect.

Now some of you skeptics are going to say, "How can that be? If a supernova happens a million light years away, it is going to take a million years to reach us. How can that supernova affect the atoms of our bodies today? It just can't happen."

In one sense, the people who say this are exactly right. When a star explodes, its matter is ejected out into space, and it will take time for that matter to reach us, a million years to be exact. But you also have to consider what created that star, what is its essence—Consciousness. When that star exploded, it not only sent shock waves across the space-time continuum, but it also sent ripples through Consciousness, and since Consciousness is infinite and everywhere at once, those ripples were felt everywhere at once, right down to the elemental particles themselves. It's a 'star explodes a neuron vibrates' type of reality.

Remember when you stubbed your toe. The reason why everything was so immediate was because your Consciousness was there. When your toe struck the table leg, your Consciousness screamed ouch!!! and all the particles in your body responded immediately. When Consciousness speaks, particles listen.

With electrons continuously blinking in and of the space-time continuum and in and out of the Infinite, they are always in constant contact with the whole universe, feeling the rippling effects coming in from everywhere. In the 'blinking out' stage, electrons are experiencing all the effects at once via Consciousness; in the 'blinking in' stage, they are responding to those effects by changing orbits within the space-time continuum. So the next time you hear about electrons jumping orbits, the next time you experience a chaotic moment or a calm moment, don't think about how random everything is, think about what is going on in the universe at that exact moment. Say to yourself, "What is going on inside this cosmic body of mine?" I believe you will find not randomness going on but a meaningful, purposeful response to all the countless activities going on within the Sea of Consciousness.

One final note. If you're wondering what stirs up the universe or quiets it down, it's Consciousness. Consciousness is the essence of all elemental particles, flows through all elemental particles. Every once and a while Consciousness likes to shake them all up, only to quiet them all down. It is all part of the process, part of the journey, that takes us all back home to the Infinite.

You probably never thought electronic orbiting could be so interesting. I'll admit none of my theories are based on any scientific fact. They are based on my own intuition, and that alone. My instincts told me to write them down, and so I did. My instincts also told me to write this book. Only time will tell how good my instincts really are.

I know a lot of what I said in this chapter is contrary to what most people believe. Some of you might be troubled, even horrified, by the fact that I'm claiming we are all...well, God. Such an idea must shake the very foundation of your religious beliefs. You must see me as a blasphemous idiot, a crazed lunatic, ready for the loony bin. Some of you might even go as far as to say I'm the Son of Satan...ouch.

All of these feelings are quite understandable given the fact our brains our operating at around 10% capacity. A Being operating at 100% capacity must seem as far removed and distant as a being can possibly be. Of course He is going to seem separate and distinct from us. "There's no way we can become That," we say. "We are just finite little creatures, while He's an Infinite Being. No way, my friend, no way." But as we grow in Consciousness, the line between our Consciousness and God's Consciousness will become more and more blurred until the distinction is at best foggy. Then even that will dissipate, leaving no distance whatsoever between us and God. We will become one with Him at that moment, and all that will be left to do will be to experience His Divine State of Being.

Why is this so troubling to some of you? All God is trying to do is give us the greatest gift He could possibly give us—Himself. What's wrong with that? Accept His gift. Weren't you taught as a young child that it was rude to turn down a gift—and you're going to turn down God's! How dare you! Come on, people, let's get with the program. It's our duty as loyal, conscious beings to obey the command of the

Highest State of Consciousness. And the command is simple: become

It.

After a hard day at the office, isn't it nice to come home to a

soothing environment, to a relaxing situation. That's all God is doing

here. He is giving us a permanent place to come home to after the long,

arduous journey. Climbing the spiritual path all the way to the pinnacle

of Being is the most difficult task in all eternity. It only seems fitting

that it reaps the greatest reward—Infinity.

CHAPTER 7

SPACE, TIME, GOD, AND NOTHINGNESS

For the most part, scientists probably don't accept what I'm saying. The reason why they don't accept it is because they don't see what I'm talking about. I'm not saying they don't get it, I'm saying they don't see it—literally. To a scientist, if it can't be seen through a microscope or a telescope, if it can't be perceived by the senses or put into a mathematical formula, then it doesn't exist. I can understand this thinking because scientists deal with the finite, not the Infinite. Their scientific instruments will never be able to detect or embrace the Infinite because the Infinite is infinitely beyond the range and scope of scientific analysis. The only way Its existence is ever verified is through a direct conscious experience. Consciousness, and Consciousness alone, is the only way to enter this Reality, the only Instrument that can fathom Its depths. If scientists want to embrace the Light, then they are going to have to fine-tune that Instrument peering through their eyes.

To make clear what I'm saying, I would like to walk you through a thought experiment. This experiment will do two things: it will show how difficult it is to perceive the Infinite, and it will show the ultimate ability of Consciousness when it comes to space and time. Our experiment is as follows:

Two scientists by the names of Bill and Fred have an isolation tank in their laboratory; they also have a high-tech machine that can determine the shape, size and speed of any object that is put inside the tank. Fred is in charge of the machine, and Bill is in charge of the tank. To make the experiment work, Fred is not allowed to watch while Bill puts objects inside the tank. This way Fred will have to rely on the machine to figure out what's inside. The experiment begins when Bill throws four tennis balls into the tank and closes the door. He then turns to Fred and asks him if he knows what's inside the tank. Fred turns the machine on and he sees there are four spherical objects that are around three inches in diameter. He tells this to Bill, and Bill says, "Correct." Bill removes the tennis balls from the tank and quietly fills it up with water. He then asks Fred if he knows what's inside the tank now. Fred looks at the machine and says, "Nice try, Billy boy, but you can't fool me. You didn't put anything in the tank. There's nothing there." Bill smiles: "O yea, why don't you come over here and open the door and see if there is anything in there or not." Fred obliges. When he opens the door, the flood-gates open and Fred becomes soaking wet. "My God!" he screams. "There was something there after all!"

What appeared to look like nothing to Fred was actually a substance that filled up the whole tank. Why Fred couldn't see it is because it didn't have any shape or size to its existence; it was basically formless. And this is the exact same problem we have when we are dealing with the Infinite. The universe is filled with countless objects of Consciousness, but Consciousness is nowhere to be seen. It has no distinguishing characteristics, no shape, size or form we can recognize. The only way we can ever see Consciousness, that is, God, is by opening the door to the depths of our Consciousness. It is there where our being will be flooded by the White Light of Consciousness, and we will know of His Existence once and for all. Until then, God will always look like nothing to us, and this is what gives some people the notion that He doesn't exist. But once the flood-gates open, we will all become soaking wet. There will be no denying His Existence then.

Now back to our experiment. After Fred puts on some dry clothes, Bill throws the same four tennis balls back into the tank, but this time he adds a fly to the mix. He asks Fred what does he see, and Fred says there are the same four spherical objects plus a tiny critter that moves around 10 ft. per second. What's peculiar about this situation is that we now have an object that moves. How is that possible? This isn't a difficult question. It's a very simple question with a very simple answer. We don't need to be experts in wing design, know about aerospace engineering or anything of the sort. That's more information than we need. The answer is much more basic than that. The reason why the fly can move is because he's...finite! Being finite, the fly can only be at one place at a time. If the fly is at point A and he wants to go to point B, he has to travel across space to get there, and it takes time to traverse that space. Thus the 10 ft. per second.

But what happens when we put water back into the tank? We find that the water is unable to move from point A to point B. Why? Because it is at both points simultaneously—it's everywhere at once! It doesn't need to move; it's already there, wherever there is.

Likewise, the Infinite functions in the same manner; It's everywhere in the universe now. We can never detect Its movement because It never moves. Only finite beings move, not the Infinite. If the Infinite could move, that would mean there is space beyond the Infinite, which means there would be a boundary line to the Infinite, and we all know there can be boundaries to the Infinite. Thus no movement.

To make my point a little clearer, try to imagine God as the fattest Being in the universe. Sorry, God, but I'm trying to make a point here. God is so fat that His Being extends to all four corners of the universe. He can't move; He's stuck. He's like an 8 by 10 slab of stone in an 8 by 10 room. So how does God get from one end of the universe to the other—through Consciousness? No need to move; His Consciousness is already there.

Now if trying to imagine God as a really fat Being is too unpleasant of an experience for you, then let's make a few changes to our thought experiment and approach it from a slightly different angle. Let's say the human body represents the universe, and an ant represents a finite state of Consciousness. The ant is going to explore every square inch of the human body, and what's unique about this ant is that every square inch he explores he retains within his Consciousness. He starts at the baby toe, then the foot, the leg, moves up the torso, the neck, face, all the way to the crown of the head. Once there the journey is over.

Now what can we determine about the ant's ability once he makes it to the crown of the head? What we can determine is that he can go anywhere he wants to via Consciousness. If he wants to go to the baby toe, he's there now; if he wants to go to the knee cap, he's there now; if he wants to go to the stomach, he's there now; if he wants to go to the nose, he's there now; if he wants to go to the crown of the head, he's there now. The reason he is able to do this is because he has become completely aware of the whole body; his Consciousness is everywhere at once.

Go ahead and try this yourself. If you direct your awareness to your little toe—you're there! If you direct your awareness to your thigh—you're there! If you direct your awareness to your belly button—you're there! If you direct your awareness to the nape of your neck—you're there! If you direct your awareness to the hair on your head—you're there!

This is exactly how it works when it comes to Consciousness and the universe. The whole universe exists within Consciousness. If the baby toe represents one end of the universe, Consciousness is there now. If the crown of the head represents the other end of the universe, Consciousness is there too. No movement is necessary. And since there is no movement, it takes no time for Consciousness to get to either location: it's instantaneous. If there was movement, then it would take time, because only finite beings can move, and it takes time for a finite being to get from one place to another. But with Consciousness, It can be wherever It wants to be—now!

If you think what I've just said is bizarre, think again; it's going to get a lot more bizarre than this, a lot more. Why I say this is because we aren't talking about a space continuum here, we are talking about a space-time continuum. Our baby toe represents not only one end of the universe, but also the beginning of time, the Big Bang. The crown of the head represents the end of time, our entrance into the Infinite. What this all means is that the whole universe, from beginning to end, is going on right now within Consciousness. The Big Bang is happening now, now is happening now, the future is happening now, the end of the universe is happening now. To deny this is to put boundaries around Consciousness; you're saying Consciousness is here but not there, is in the present but not in the past or future, but we already know Consciousness is infinite and thus is everywhere at once. This has to apply to time as well as to space.

I know what I've just said is totally incomprehensible. Being in a finite state of Consciousness, we can only see the universe within a sequential time frame, that is, past, present, and future: we are here but not there. To an Infinite Being, though, it is all happening NOW. We will never be able to fully grasp or comprehend this until we become Infinite ourselves. Until then, we must put our faith in Infinity's Logic; it's flawless.

This new insight into time, though, does help explain a few oddities out there. One such oddity is the ability to see into the future. Why some people are able to do this is because the future is already happening somewhere within Consciousness. One curiosity of mine I've had over the years is that I've never been able to figure out what God did the first ten billion years of this universe. Yes, He slowly formed galaxies out of gaseous clouds, created stars, planets, moons, asteroids, comets and so forth, but during all this time there were no conscious beings of any kind exploring this universe. So what did He do? I thought He would eventually go stir crazy if all He did over the eons was create celestial bodies and watch them go round and around and around and around. But now I get it. The past, present, and future don't exist in God's State of Consciousness; it's all happening at once within His Being. The gaseous cloud formations, the star formations, the planet formations are all happening now, just as we're happening now.

Throughout this book I have mentioned many a time that Consciousness is the source and essence of all creation; not one particle of existence can be reduced to anything less than Consciousness. When this universe ends, it will dissolve back into Consciousness, and one of the main attributes of Consciousness is awareness. Thus, Consciousness will always be aware of every moment of time, because every moment of time can be reduced to Consciousness. This is how God can be at the Big Bang and the end of the universe simultaneously. Both moments are moments of time whose essence is Consciousness, and Consciousness is always aware of every moment of time—always.

To show you that we have the ability to do this, I would like to introduce you to Wilder Penfield, a famous neurosurgeon who passed away in the 1970's. Before he died, he wrote an interesting book called 'The Mystery Of The Mind.' In this book he talked about some of his most bizarre moments as a neurosurgeon, and one of his favorites had to do with patients who remained awake during brain surgery. (This is easy to do because the brain feels no pain.) What he discovered was that whenever he targeted a very specific area of their brains and stimulated it, his patients would always tell him at that exact moment of stimulation that they were experiencing a past moment in their lives. At first, Dr. Penfield dismissed this as mere memories from the past, but after hearing one patient after another give an emphatic 'no' to that, he soon realized something else was going on: his patients weren't remembering the past, they were experiencing the past—literally. To paraphrase one patient: "They weren't memories at all. It was like I was actually there, reliving a moment in my life." This, as you can well see, is a perfect example of what I mean when I say every moment of time can be reduced to Consciousness.

Of course, skeptics will say, "The brain made it happen." Well, if that's the case, then I have only one question for you skeptics: where did the brain come from? It came from the same place everything else comes from—God, that is, Consciousness. Consciousness doesn't need the brain to exist for It to exist; It's been doing just fine existing forever on Its own, thank you. The brain, on the other hand, does need Consciousness to exist for it to exist; otherwise there would be no brain. Yes, it's true, the brain has the ability to access Consciousness, but it can't create Consciousness; it can't create something that's uncreated. Take away the brain and Consciousness would still be; take away Consciousness and only nothing would be. A world renowned scientist by the name of Carl Sagan once said: "Consciousness is the epiphenomenon of the brain." I beg to differ: the brain is the epiphenomenon of Consciousness. (Not bad for a cab driver, don't you think? I mean, you know, taking on Carl Sagan and all.)

Now that I've completely turned your world upside down, it gets even crazier. I have also shown in this book that there are infinite universes out there, which means, you guessed it, all infinite universes are going on now, all probability waves have collapsed at once. Trying to comprehend this is beyond our state of Consciousness, but here is an image for you that might help. When we stand in front of an ocean, we are looking out at zillions and zillions of water molecules, and all those water molecules are existing now. That's God. He is a Sea of Infinite Consciousness, filled with infinite universes, and His Consciousness is flowing through all those universes now. If it wasn't this way, then there would be boundaries, and do I even need to bother telling you anymore what that means?

A fun way to describe what I'm saying here is to imagine God as a Hollywood director. When we go to a movie, we have no idea how it's going to begin, where it's going to go, or how it's going to end. The director, on the other hand, not only knows everything about the movie, but he's already seen it from beginning to end. Our God is one such Director. He has made infinite movies, and they are all being shown now in His Moviehouse, with continuous showings throughout eternity. All this is possible because every moment of time, every frame of existence, is always there within Consciousness; it always was there, always is there, and always will be there forever and ever.

Now some of you are probably saying to yourself, "What's the point? If it's already a done deal, why do anything?" First, go ahead and try to do nothing and see how long you can do it for. I guarantee you you won't be able to do it forever. Something is eventually going to stir you to action, and that something is Consciousness. And second, never forget what the other half of God's Infinity is: to experience infinite experiences. The only way God can experience infinite experiences is to explore infinite universes. The only way God can explore infinite universes is to become finite, that is, to become us. Once He becomes us, He is able to move through a universe, but it takes time for a finite being to move, and since there are infinite universes out there, it is going to take an infinite amount of time to explore an infinite amount of universes. This is how it has to be if God is to complete His Infinity.

What I have just described is the ultimate paradox of God and time. In one state, the infinite state, God is able to see all of eternity now; in another state, the finite state, it is going to take Him forever to see it all. It's nuts, I know, but what do you expect from God: He's incomprehensible. We will never be able to fathom His Divine Being from a finite perspective. We will need to become Him to comprehend Him. And this will always happen, because we can never escape our Essence, and our Essence is God.

But the heck with all this. We don't need to concern ourselves with metaphysical issues like space and time. All we need concern ourselves with is now, the present moment, what the Zen Buddhists call the Eternal Present. Being finite we can only be at one place at a time, and that place is the present. It is always there, and we can never escape it. Trying to do so would be like trying to run from our shadows: no matter where we run to, there's the present. This is what we will always be confronted with while we are in a finite state of being, and it will never end, for we are nothing more than a stream of Consciousness, forever lost in the Eternal Present, floating from one present moment to the next throughout all eternity.

So, so what if Consciousness is everywhere at once, so what if everything that's possible is happening now or has already happened. We will never know any of this while we are in a finite state of Consciousness. All we will ever know is the moment in front of us, nothing more. So don't worry about the fact that you are unable to fully grasp the metaphysical mysteries of space, time and God. You don't need to grasp all that now. It's not necessary. God designed eternity this way so that He can play the Consciousness Game and complete His Infinity. The mysteries will be revealed in due time; they always are. But for now, just worry about now. It's all we got—forever.

CHAPTER 8

PAIN AND SUFFERING

Being totally engrossed in writing the last two chapters, I almost forgot about our friend the atheist. The reason why I've neglected him so is because I believe I have already used the ammo necessary to blow his pompous little philosophy right out of the water. But some atheists don't give up so easily; they still have one more argument in their arsenal. It's rather a meaningless argument, but one in which they really think they 'gotcha'. Their argument goes as follows:

The atheist walks up to you and says, "O yea, if God exists, then why do good people suffer? Why is there so much pain and misery in the world if God exists? Huh! Huh!" Atheists, what a bunch of wimps. Because life is tough, there is no God? What nonsense. Did it ever occur to you, my dear atheist, that it is precisely because life is so tough that makes it so worthwhile? Did it ever occur to you that if life were easy it would be an absolute bore? Did any of this ever occur to you? Huh! Huh! I will go into this in more detail shortly, but for the moment let's give the atheist what he wants.

To make him happy, let's pretend we lived in a world where there was no sickness or disease, no crime or war, no rich or poor, where everyone loved one another and we all held hands and played 'ring around the rosy'. If we lived in such a world, do you really believe, my dear atheist, that this would put an end to all pain and suffering? If you think so, think again, for you are forgetting one irrefutable fact about our being, and it is this: we are finite.

Being finite means we have a beginning and an end to our existences, and since this is the case, we have no choice but to experience the greatest pain of all: the loss of our loved ones. There is no pain—no pain!—greater in all eternity than watching the people we love die. Those are the moments when our world stops turning and our will to live collapses. Nothing matters to us anymore; all we want to do is find a hole to crawl into and die. The pain is just too great to bear, and there is nothing we can do about it. Not even God, in all His infinite wisdom and glory, can do anything to prevent this pain from happening. Only He is infinite, only He lasts forever, only He has no beginning or end; every other form of existence must cease to exist at some point in time. There just is no way around this eternal law of being; it's inscribed in the annals of eternity, and it will remain there until eternity passes away. Until then, all things must pass, except for the Infinite One.

So what are we to make of all this? To me it's obvious: pain is inevitable, whether God exists or not. If the atheist insists on there being no pain in order for God to exist, then what does he propose we do to get around this huge obstacle in front of us? Feel nothing? That makes a lot of sense: I feel nothing, therefore God exists. Who wants to make that claim? Or maybe the atheist believes we should be able to feel love without pain if God existed. How is that supposed to work? Let's see, someone you dearly love dies and you feel no pain. How is that possible? The amount of pain you feel when someone you know dies is equal to the amount of love you felt for that person when that person was alive. No pain, no love; no love, no pain. It's that simple. If this is what the atheist wants—no pain—then what other possible way is there to experience love?

There isn't any! That's why God's plan is so perfect. He doesn't want us to mimic love, He wants us to experience love, and the only way we can experience love fully is to experience the pain of loss that comes with it; otherwise the experience would be a watered down version or some third rate mimicry of love. That's not good enough. God wants the real deal. All experiences must be authentic and must be experienced. This is the means by which God is able to complete His Infinity.

To make myself perfectly clear, I would like to share with you a line from a letter that was read during a TV documentary called 'Letters

From Vietnam'. It was a deeply moving letter written by a mother who lost her son in Vietnam. I will never forget this line as long as I live, and I am not ashamed to admit that tears are welling up in my eyes as I begin writing this short but succinct line. It goes as follows: 'Son, I just want to let you know that even with all the pain at the end, you were worth having'. What a powerful statement. This mother had to have been experiencing insufferable grief, and yet she was willing to endure it all, accept it all, for she knew that the experience of being a mother and loving a son was the greatest experience she could ever have, even with all the pain at the end. What more needs to be said. It doesn't get any more real than that. If you are looking for proof that God doesn't exist, my dear atheist, don't go looking for grieving mothers. Show me a mother who doesn't grieve and I will show you a God that doesn't exist.

Now a fair-minded atheist might say, "I would be willing to accept the pain of loss and still believe in God as long as the world is good, but since there is so much evil in the world, I cannot in good conscience believe in God." Alright, at least we are making some progress here.

The atheist is willing to accept some pain and still believe in God as long as the world is good. Let's explore this idea and see where it takes us.

If all we ever lived in was a good world, and that was all we ever knew or experienced, how would we know what we were experiencing was good? What would we have based it on? If we never saw or experienced evil, couldn't we just as easily have said our world was evil instead of good? How would we have known the difference? It is only through the interplay of opposites that we become aware of the other side; we know white because of black, light because of dark, joy because of sorrow. If we take one side out of the equation, the whole equation collapses and becomes void of any meaning. Both sides are needed for conscious development.

This is why Adam and Eve had to be tossed out of the Garden of Eden. They didn't have a clue where they were at. They could've been told they were in heaven or hell and that would have meant absolutely nothing to them because they hadn't become aware of opposites yet. They needed to enter existence and experience its hardships to learn what the Garden was all about. They had to leave it to get back to it. The eviction notice was posted on the Tree of Life and they were sent into exile to start an incredible journey, a journey that continues today through us.

God's primary objective in all this is to make sure we all evolve into the Light; everything else is secondary. This is why He allows heinous acts to happen, because they are all instrumental in stirring Consciousness to action and forcing It to move along the evolutionary path. Good and evil are nothing more than opposing forces at opposite ends of the existence pole pushing against each other, and this pushing pushes the middle upward, and the middle is Consciousness, and Consciousness is going to keep pushing upward until It finally touches the Sky of Eternal Being. It is there where all duality ends and the One remains. In other words, Consciousness has evolved into God. The journey is over.

All this was made possible because of the existence of evil. Without it, we would still be in the Garden of Eden, walking aimlessly through the tulips like mindless automatons, not having a clue what life, existence and God were all about. What an exciting adventure that would have been.

After hearing my theory on evil, our fair-minded atheist might say, "If God exists, can't He make us become aware of evil and protect us from it at the same time? Is all this pain and suffering really necessary?" In other words, he wants God to be an over protective parent. It's a nice thought—see no evil, hear no evil—but as any good parent knows, you cannot shelter your children. Sheltering them prevents them from growing, and a child needs to grow if he is going to evolve into a mature human being. God understands this all too well. He knows we need to grow to evolve, and the only way we can grow is by becoming aware. If life was never difficult, if we never went through trying times, if terrible things never happened to good people, how could we ever become aware of evil? And if we don't become aware of evil, how can we ever grow in awareness? We can't. We will always be limited, and this limitation will keep our Consciousness from evolving into God. Thus, evil must exist and must be confronted.

What I'm describing here is similar to what goes on during psychoanalysis. Any good psychoanalyst knows you never overcome your fears by running away from them or suppressing them. You need to face them, confront them, and this will allow you to grow psychically. Evil is no different. By confronting it head on, our Consciousness will grow and expand, and through this continuous expansion of Consciousness we will eventually expand into the Infinite, all because of our confrontations with evil. Yes, there will be many painful moments along the way, but there will be many great moments as well, and the totality of all these experiences will enable us to figure this whole mess out and transform it into the God-State. Just watch. But until then, we need to keep coming back until we get it right. Graduation won't happen until we all graduate together; and in order to graduate we must pass all the tests, and some of the toughest tests of all are our battles with evil.

So we might as well get used to it, evil is going to be with us every step of the way. It is as critical to existence as love, kindness and compassion are. It is the stimulus that arouses Consciousness to action and puts in motion the whole evolutionary process. Our concern, therefore, shouldn't be with the existence of evil but with how to deal with it when it comes our way. A quick look at human history and we can see how important it is to confront evil whenever it rears its ugly head.

One prime example of evil is none other than Hitler. He was a maniacal madman who wanted to rule the world. Can you imagine what this world would be like today, or better yet, what our state of Consciousness would be like if we sat idly by and did nothing to stop this guy? Would our world have been a better place to live in, would our Consciousness have grown, or would we have been reduced to nothing but a bunch of mind-numbed robots, crying "*Heil* Hitler!" when ordered to do so and having no originality to our thoughts or ideas whatsoever? I believe the answer is obvious.

Worse still, how would we have explained ourselves to history? What would our answers have been to the children of the future when they asked their history teachers, "Why did this happen? Why didn't the world fight back? Why did they let this madman conquer the world? Why did they let their civilization crumble? Why did they allow the extermination of a race of people? Was 20th century man a coward? Was he afraid to fight back? Did he run from bullies? Was he taught not to stand up for what he believed in? Why was all this necessary? Why, teacher, why?" Great questions, kids. Fortunately, we don't have to answer them; we took care of business instead. By confronting this evil tyrant, our civilization eventually grew and prospered, and more importantly, our Consciousness evolved. Yes, millions died, but as long as our Consciousness grows we know we are on the right pathway to God. After all, isn't Consciousness who we really are anyway? Our bodies may fall, but our Consciousness will always be.

Now our atheist friend is predictable here. He always asks the same question: "If God existed, why would He have allowed Hitler to exist?" Again, the atheist doesn't get it. It's not God's job to do away with evil; it's our job to confront it and defeat it whenever it appears on the horizon. Every time we do this we pass another test on our way to Godhood. Hitler was one such test, but he wasn't the first, nor is he the last. There will be more, many more, believe me. As we grow in Consciousness, evil will grow too, and as our Consciousness ascends to ever greater heights, evil's diabolical nature will become much more devious and cunning, matching our wits every step of the way.

And let's not stop with human evil; we have our enemies in the micro-world as well. Diseases such as smallpox and the bubonic plague ravaged the human race, killing millions of people. Consciousness was forced to act; It had to probe deeper into the molecular structure of our being to find new ways to fight those diseases. Eventually Consciousness found those ways, and in the process It became more aware of the micro-world and thus grew. Now we have a new menace called AIDS; it too has killed millions of people. Once again Consciousness is hard at work trying desperately to find a new way to capture and destroy this illusive virus. In time Consciousness will succeed in Its endeavor, but do you really think AIDS will be the last toxic microbe to invade the human race? Of course not. As our Consciousness grows and becomes more complex, so will the micro-killers, giving Consciousness more headaches to deal with, challenging It to create new and better weaponry to fight these noxious, pathogenic evildoers.

And let's not stop here either. We have our disasters, or evils, in the natural world too. Events like earthquakes, hurricanes, tornadoes, volcanoes, floods, drought and so forth wreak havoc on the human populace, causing all kinds of problems for Consciousness. These problems are necessary, though, because they keep Consciousness active, alert, sharp and in shape so that It can always be ready to flex Its muscle whenever or wherever another hardship arises. It is a never-ending battle, all the way to the end.

Without these battles or hardships, Consciousness would remain in a dormant state, incapable of ever growing towards the Light. We need to become the Light; it is our destiny; and in order to get there we need to show we are worthy of It, that we have what it takes to become It. It is one thing to say you're courageous, but until you actually show it on the battlefield, how will you ever really know for sure? This is what God wants to find out. He wants to know if we have the mettle and character to become Him. He doesn't want some sap at the pearly-gates; He wants His equal; and to become His equal we need to show we are capable of handling any situation, no matter how hard the hardship. This is how we cross over into the Infinite, where our Consciousness and God's Consciousness become one and the same.

When it comes right down to it, there is no other way for God to run His universes. Believe me, if He could, He would. God isn't some type of sadomasochist who likes to inflict all this pain and suffering on us, but He understands better than anyone that to evolve His creation back into Himself, the dark side of existence must be assimilated into His Being. By assimilating the dark side, Consciousness becomes whole, complete, and is able to enter the Divine State of Being. But until the process of assimilation has been fully completed, we will never be able to handle the full Force of God. We would be like a moth to a flame, consumed in an instant; but by evolving into the Flame, we will have avoided being torched. This is what all our battles with evil are preparing us for, grooming us for: to become the Eternal Flame.

I can see it all now. Way into the future at the end of the universe the ultimate battle between Good and Evil will arise. One choice will destroy the whole universe; the other will transform it into the Light. What do you think will happen? The answer is rather obvious, don't you think?

Now I don't want to leave you with the impression that I'm saying there is an absolute Evil out there somewhere, *i.e.* Satan. I am not saying that at all. Remember what I said at the beginning of the book: all that is happening is God, and God alone. God plays all the roles; He is the Face behind all the masks. He is the saint and the sinner, the genius and the madman, the cop and the robber, the good guy and the bad guy, the psychiatrist and the psychopath, all at the same time. While He is playing these roles, His Consciousness is in a finite state, and thus He can only be aware of the role He's playing. A lot of these roles will clash with each other, but it is through these clashes that Consciousness grows and expands and eventually finds Its way back Home. And never forget what the other half of God's Infinity is: to experience infinite experiences. By playing infinite roles, He experiences infinite experiences, and all these experiences are designed to slowly evolve Consciousness back into the Infinite. It is a perfectly laid out plan, a plan that only God could have come up with.

So let not your heart be troubled; all the pain and suffering we are going through will pay off in the end. Accomplishing anything worthwhile takes a lot of time and effort, and there will always be setbacks and hardships along the way. That's what makes it so worthwhile. If anyone could win a gold medal, then what value would there be in a gold medal? There wouldn't be any. The extreme sacrifices athletes make to have a chance at winning the gold is what makes it so special, and when one is fortunate enough to win the gold, he won't be standing around whining and complaining how difficult it was to win it; rather, he will be standing proud and erect, relishing the moment, cherishing it, glad that he hung in there to the end so that he could experience this glorious moment in his life. Being the best was worth the sacrifice, and the pain and agony he had to endure to become number one is now nothing more than a fading memory. Likewise, Consciousness has to make the same sacrifices to go for Its Gold. Becoming God is the greatest experience of all; therefore, we will have to experience the greatest hardships of all to become Him. Once we make it, though, and the lights of eternity shine upon us, we won't be dwelling on all the crimes and wars and sicknesses and diseases and disasters and turmoils we had to go through to get there. Instead, we will be focusing all our attention on the gloriousness of our Being, praising eternity for our victory, realizing once and for all we are God Almighty, the Creator and Master of all. So hang in there, we will get through this. We always do.

CHAPTER 9

CONCLUSION

So have I done it? Has this cab driver from Tucson, Arizona proven

beyond the shadow of a doubt the existence of God? Have I pounded

the final nail in the atheist's coffin? Have I rid the world of his

obnoxious philosophy once and for all? Is it now a philosophy of the

past and nothing more? Who I am to say; I'm the last one to be

objective here. Like a mother who can find no fault with her child, I

can find no fault with my book; it's just too close to my heart. It is going to have to be up to you to decide. You are the final arbitrators on deciding whether my book lives or dies, whether it becomes part of human Consciousness or part of the useless debris inside my closet, condemned to a life of gathering dust on its yellowing pages until the day I die. Then it can be burned. Only time will tell how it all plays out. In the meantime, all I can do is hope for the best and leave the rest to God, that deepest layer of Consciousness existing somewhere within my being. (Are you listening God? Can you hear me? I could use some help here, if you know what I mean. Couldn't you silently influence the Consciousness of one or two publishers and make them become extremely interested in my book? I sure would appreciate it. Hey, what have I got to lose, I need all the help I can get. Anyway, a little imploring never hurt anyone.)

I would, however, like to make one final apology for my argument. Why I think my idea is so unique is because I don't take the standard route. Love, order in the universe, symmetry in nature, intelligent design have always been the arguments used in proving the existence of God, but love, order, symmetry, and design have never been definitive proofs that God exists. The atheist has always been able to find a way to weasel his way out of these arguments. A new approach was needed, and I believe I have found it. Instead of focusing on the behavior of existence, I focused on existence itself—why is it even here to begin with? And what I discovered was Infinity Itself.

Unfortunately, this discovery of mine shouldn't be such a novel idea. I don't know what it is, but whenever we mention Infinity we act like our mind has run into a brick wall. I don't get it. I guess it's because we feel Infinity is beyond our scope of intelligence and there's nothing we can do about it: God is infinite and we're not and that's that. But what does it mean to be infinite? We know it means to exist forever, but what's been going on within that 'foreverness?' That's the wall our brain cells run into every time we contemplate Infinity. We've never really thought it through.

One of the main reasons why we haven't thought it through is because we are too caught up in our own universe; we are so in awe of it that we never look beyond it. We never wonder what went on for all eternity before our universe came into being, and we never wonder what will go on for all eternity once our universe ceases to exist. Instead, we ask questions like "Does the universe go on forever? Is it infinite or finite?", but these are the wrong questions to ask. It's not whether our universe goes on forever or not, it's not whether it's infinite or not, it's whether Consciousness is infinite or not, and I have shown that Consciousness has to be infinite. Since we now know Consciousness is our Infinite Being, and since there can be only one Infinite Being, everything else has to be finite, including our universe. As incomprehensibly amazing as our universe is, it is nothing compared to Infinity. It is a mere speck of existence within an infinity of specks, creating a plenum of existence that spans eternity. This is the Infinity in which I discovered.

The only alternative to this Infinity is to say there are a finite number of universes, but that creates the 'first universe' dilemma: how does nothing exist forever first, then creates a first universe? It can't happen. Since it takes forever for forever to come to an end, nothingness would be the only existence in all eternity, and it would have to remain that way forever. Unless you can find a way to bring forever to an end, this is the way it would have to be—forever.

In retrospect, there have always been two potential infinities: an infinity of nothingness, and an infinity of being. If there was an infinity of nothingness, you and I wouldn't be here; since you and I are here, there has to be an infinity of being. Only one can win out, and being is the winner.

All I am using here in proving the existence of an existential Infinity is a form of inductive reasoning. From this one particular example—our universe—we can induce that there are infinite universes out there. To have one existence is to have infinite existences. We don't need to discover infinite universes to prove this point; all we need to do is discover one and we can infer that the rest exist. From the experience of one, we have found the many.

Why has this been so difficult to figure out? I am not talking rocket science here. We don't need to be experts in mathematics or physics to fathom Infinity. All we need is a little intellect and a lot of common sense. Existence has been around forever, and thus it has to be sustained by a Being who exists forever, *i.e.* God. What's so complicated about that? This is the way forever has to be. It can't be any other way. Go ahead and try to find another forever and see what happens. What you will find is that menacing 'first universe' problem lurking at every turn. Good luck in your search.

Another shocker my argument makes is that I claim we are the proprietors of this Infinity. I have shown that the Consciousness peering through our eyes is the same Consciousness as the one that creates and sustains infinite universes. We don't realize this yet because we are in a finite state of Consciousness, but we are heading headlong towards the Source, and it will be only a matter of time before we find ourselves flowing into an Ocean of Light.

I know I lose a lot of you when I say this. The reason why I lose you is because you find comfort in worshipping and praying to a Being greater than yourself, and the idea you are this Being is beyond your wildest imagination. That's okay. The fact that you are acknowledging God is what's important here. We all need guidance and direction, and

God is the best Guide of all. Where you and I differ is in the perception

of Him: you see Him as a Being separate from us; I see Him as our

deepest layer of Consciousness waiting to be discovered. Until we

know for sure, until the day of reckoning is upon us, let's keep our

options open and see what the future holds. You might find that this

Being you are worshipping and praying to, whether it be in a church,

temple, synagogue or mosque, is really nothing but a mirror, reflecting

the true Infinity of our Being. Only time will tell if there is a reflection

or not.

Another area of disagreement you and I might have when it comes

to God is this idea of heaven and hell. Since you believe God is

separate from us, you believe He is going to send us to a permanent

place after we die: heaven if we were good, hell if we were bad. I'm

sorry, but I don't understand this type of thinking. I don't mean to be

rude here, but I don't think you've really thought this idea through

either; the logic behind it is appalling. Before you were born, there was

a forever when you didn't exist, and now you're going to exist forever

after you die. How is that possible? It makes no sense whatsoever and it perverts the true meaning of forever. You can't start existing forever anymore than you can stop existing forever. If you exist forever, then you exist forever: you always were, always are, and always will be forever and ever. End of story.

What we have here is a problem similar to the first universe problem. If we didn't exist forever, then how could we ever come into existence? We couldn't. The only reason we are here now is because we have always existed, and there is only one Being who exists forever—God. That's who we are. We are God Incarnate. We are the Being who peers through our eyes, who hides behind our masks, who disguises Himself in an infinite variety of ways so that He can play infinite roles, explore infinite worlds, experience infinite experiences. This is God. This is us. This is forever.

So what do I make of heaven and hell then? I see them as being nothing more than motivational techniques sent down from the Divine. Haven't you ever heard parents say to their kids, "I brought you into this world, I can take you out of this world" or "I am going to ground you for life for doing that!" You know they really don't mean it when they make statements like that, but they say them in the hope of keeping their children on the 'straight and narrow' so that they don't make the same mistakes in the future. God is no different. He wants you to lead a spiritual life, and there is nothing like the threat of eternal damnation to get your attention. But as you grow spiritually, your interest in heaven and hell slowly wanes. You begin to realize you walk the spiritual path, not because you fear hell or desire heaven, but because it is the right thing to do. You want to live a righteous life, and the spiritual way is the only way to live righteously. Once you come to this realization, heaven and hell mean absolutely nothing to you anymore. All that matters is walking the walk and living each moment in a Godlike fashion. You seek nothing more, want nothing less. Punishment becomes nothing more than straying from the path; reward becomes nothing more than staying on the path. And when the time comes when we all stay on the path and walk righteously together, we will be able to universalize our Consciousness and bring this universe of ours to fruition. So if heaven and hell have any importance at all, it is to set us on the path of righteousness, and thus to Infinity.

Does this mean, then, heaven and hell don't exist? I will never make such a claim for the simple reason I will never put limits on Consciousness. Consciousness can create whatever It wants to create. Like the *yogi* who created a palace for his disciple, Consciousness can create heaven and hell for us. Maybe Dante did experience 'The *Inferno*,' 'The *Purgatorio*,' and 'The *Paradisio*,' but even if he did, those places, like all places, come from Consciousness and return to Consciousness. They couldn't exist forever anymore than you, I, or this universe could. All things must pass, except for Consciousness. So who's to say if heaven and hell exist or not? It's quite possible they do exist, but exist forever, now that's impossible.

As I come to the end of my book, I realize now that I haven't been writing my philosophy but God's philosophy. I know it sounds arrogant to say I've gone inside the Mind of God, but it isn't as difficult as you might think. Go ahead and try it yourself and see what you find. If you were God and you could create a universe, wouldn't you do so; and if you could create a universe, wouldn't you want to explore that universe; and if you could explore that universe, would you want to know you were God while doing it? What fun would that be? You would be bored out of your gourd. Knowing all takes the adventure out of the adventure, the mystery out of the mystery, the suspense out of the suspense. Not knowing is what makes the journey so incredibly exciting and interesting; it's what keeps you involved in the Game until the end. This is why God does what He does. He loses Himself in His creation so that He can experience everything possible, explore everything possible. Existence to Him becomes nothing more than one great big feast waiting to be devoured. Like red ants consuming their prey until it's gone, His voracious Consciousness consumes existence until there is nothing left but a Supreme Being! Now that's a feast. If this sounds pleasing to your palate, then you've entered the Mind of God and grasped His philosophy of being: devour it until your petite little Consciousness becomes the Supreme Consciousness you always were. If this sounds too unsavory to you, if it leaves a foul taste in your mouth, then please show me where I have gone wrong in explaining God's philosophy because I don't see it.

Before I close up shop, I would like to make one final comment about Consciousness. If you still don't believe that what peers through your eyes is God, then what you are saying, in essence, is that Consciousness isn't infinite. If you believe this, then there had to be a point in eternity when Consciousness didn't exist, and that point had to exist forever. Since it takes forever for forever to come to an end...you get the point, Consciousness could never have come into existence. Thus, by simply using the magnificent technique of inductive reasoning, we can easily determine that since we are having are moment in the Sun now, the Sun has always shone. And who's the Sun...we are.

Why some of you God believers have such a difficult time accepting all this is because you believe in God, and thus God Consciousness, but you don't believe our Consciousness can become God Consciousness. Well, if everything comes from God, then everything returns to God. All of existence, from atoms to stars, from galaxies to universes, eventually dissolves back into the Consciousness of God. We can't help but become It; every particle of existence becomes It. Like a mirage fading into the hot Sahara desert, our universe will one day fade away into Infinite Being. Simply put, we are nothing but a dream that is slowly transforming itself into the Being dreaming the dream. So we might as well get use to it, folks, we are the Dreamer. Why fight it.

In closing, all I have really done in this book is give you a cartographical experience: I have drawn for you the map of God, but I am unable to show you how to get there. It's one thing to draw a map of Everest, it's quite another to climb it. Climbing the spiritual mountain all the way to the pinnacle of Being is the greatest challenge of all, and this is the task we've undertaken. I'm sorry, but I'm not the one to be your guide because I am as screwed up as the rest of you. But together we can find a pathway to the Summit, where the glorious White Light of Divinity awaits our entrance. So let's put on our climbing shoes and start climbing. No storm is too big, no avalanche too tough to keep us form our appointed destiny. The Light awaits us, and we are inching our way there with every step we make. So hang in there, people, we will make it. We always do.

Well, I'm finished. I have nothing more to say or do. Either I have convinced you or I haven't, either I write well or I don't, either this book is ready for human consumption or it's not. Only time will tell. But if this book isn't meant for the light of day, if it's meant to be a dust-grabber and nothing more, then I have only one question for You God—why? Why did You put this idea in my head in the first place, why did You make me live and breathe it for almost three years, why did You make me walk hundreds, if not thousands, of miles thinking about it, why did You make me agonize over every semi-colon, adverb, and verb tense when You knew I couldn't write, and more importantly, why did You make me write about You when You knew no one was going to read it, why, God, why? I guess you have your reasons, but God, just so that You know; I really hate to dust....

THE END

COPYRIGHT

Library of Congress Control Number: 2011910030.

EPub Edition © June 2011 ISBN–10: 0615497713
EPub Edition © June 2011 ISBN–13: 978–0–615–49771–6

Print Edition © November 2011 ISBN–10: 0615570755
Print Edition © November 2011 ISBN–13: 978–0–615–57075–4

FIRST PRINT EDITION

10 9 8 7 6 5 4 3 2 1

ABOUT THE AUTHOR

Stephen J. Franey

Steve was born on April 6, 1955 and has called Tucson, Arizona, his home for many years. An avid outdoorsman, he is never closer to God than when he walks in his favorite forests spots vacationing in Idaho and Montana. On his trips to the national forests he is always accompanied by his "bestest bud," an adventure cat, aptly named, Montana.

Made in the USA
Las Vegas, NV
19 June 2022

50444920R00098